WEAPONS OF MASS CONFIDENCE:

HOW AI WILL HELP WOMEN WIN MORE

Kat Thomas

WHAT PEOPLE ARE SAYING ABOUT WEAPONS OF MASS CONFIDENCE:

"Such a timely and much needed confidence booster, especially for women, in a time of uncertainty. Kat confirms my belief that AI may well end up being the best actor in a supporting role, but it will never deliver the leading performance. Humans will always be best placed to do that!"
HOLLY BRANSON VIRGIN CHIEF PURPOSE AND VISION OFFICER

"AI is the friend all women need. Don't be scared, be excited. Don't be shut out... get in there now, while it's still young enough for us to have a hand in its creation. AI's future must have Mothers as well as Fathers"
CAROLINE QUENTIN - ACTRESS, BROADCASTER AND TELEVISION PRESENTER

"This idea is all about crucial optimism... it's AI, giving women a simple steer, to help us feel more confident in decision-making, with warmth and possibility. It's about time."
EMMA FREUD - BROADCASTER, JOURNALIST AND PRODUCER

"AI can be a great leveller, but only if women feel confident enough to question it, use it and collectively contribute to it to shape what comes next. It's exciting times and AI can help in so many ways, it has been incredibly important for my new business and has enabled me to do things that I only dreamt of."
JODIE KIDD - TV PERSONALITY AND ENTREPRENEUR

"I love the idea of women using new tools like AI to feel more confident in their everyday lives. Anything that helps women back themselves is worth paying attention to."
NICKY ZIMMERMANN, ZIMMERMANN CREATIVE DIRECTOR AND CO FOUNDER

"My work has shown me how quickly women can lose trust in themselves when they're the target of scams and intimate abuse. Confidence is often the first casualty when you've experienced grooming, manipulation and worse. What I admire about Kat's approach in Weapons of Mass Confidence is the way she reframes technology as something that can actually help women regain that trust - in their instincts, in their decision-making, and in their right to ask questions before something goes wrong. This book offers women a way to step back into their power at a time when the digital world is becoming more complicated than ever."

TRACY HALL, AUTHOR, SPEAKER, ADVOCATE AND EDUCATOR - SCAMS AND INTIMATE FRAUD

Text copyright © Kat Thomas 2026
Design copyright © Kat Thomas 2026
All rights reserved.

Kat Thomas has asserted her right under the Copyright, Designs and Patents Act 1988 to be identified as the author of this work.

No part of this book may be reprinted or reproduced or utilised in any form or by electronic, mechanical or any other means, now known or hereafter invented, including photocopying or recording, or in any information storage or retrieval system, without the permission in writing from the Publisher and Author.

Although the author and publisher have made every effort to ensure that the information in this book was correct at the time of publication, the author and publisher do not assume and hereby disclaim any liability to any party for loss, damage or disruption caused by errors or omissions, whether such errors or omissions result from negligence, accident or any other cause.

First published 2026
by Rowanvale Books Ltd
The Gate
Keppoch Street
Roath
Cardiff
CF24 3JW
www.rowanvalebooks.com

A CIP catalogue record for this book is available from the British Library.
Paperback ISBN: 978-1-83584-202-7
eBook ISBN: 978-1-83584-201-0

Printed and bound by CPI Group (UK) Ltd, Croydon, CR0 4YY

DEDICATED TO ALL THE ABSOLUTE LEGENDS I'VE KNOWN, PAST AND PRESENT:

Aideen, Agnes, Aimee, Aislinn, Al, Alana, Alia, Alice, Alison, Aline, Amara, Amelia, Amber, Amity, Amy, Andie, Angela, Anna, Annamaria, Annie, Ari, Bec, Belinda, Bipsha, Briony, Calli, Camille, Candice, Cara, Caroline, Casey, Cat, Cath, Catherine, Caitlin, Charis, Charla, Charlie, Charlotte, Cherry, Christine, Claire, Clare, Colette, Corinna, Cressida, Daniella, Danielle, Deborah, Deepa, Dian, Dilys, Dobster, Dorothy, Elektra, Elenor, Emily, Emma, Emmalago, Erin, Fenella, Felicity, Fiona, Fleur, Frankie, Francis, Georgia, Georgie, Grace, Hadas, Hannah, Harkiran, Hayley, Heidi, Hélène, Helen, Hollie, Ife, Imogen, Indianna, Ioana, Jackie, Jade, Jamie, Janna, Jeanne-Marie, Jemma, Jenna, Jennifer, Jenny, Jess, Jessica, Jill, Jingwei, Jo, Jodi, Jodie, Joelle, Joy, Judilicious, Jude, Julia, Julie, Kara, Karen, Karynne, Kate, Katie, KeeKee, Kelly, Kerri, Kieran, Kimmie, Kirsty, Laila, Laura, Lauren, Leila, Lené, Leonora, Letitia, Libby, Ling, Linsay, Lisa, Liv, Liz, Lizzie, Lizzy, Lou, Louisa, Louise, Lucinda, Lucy, Maddie, Maddy, Maggie, Maisie, Margy, Mariella, Marissa, Mary, Matea, Maur, May, MC, Meghan, Megan, Melanie, Melissa, Meryl, Michaela, Michelle, Midori, Minal, Miranda, Misha, Mollie, Nadia, Naomi, Natalie, Natasha, Nelly, Nicole, Nicky, Niki, Nikki, Nina, Nornifa, Nuala, Odette, Olga, Olivia, Pam, Pamela, Parris, Patricia, Patti, Pechey, Pia, Rachael, Rebecca, Rhiannon, Ros, Rosie, Roz, Sadie, Sally, Sam, Sama, Samantha, Sammy, Sarah, Sarika, Sars, Serina, Sharnece, Shirley, Siobhan, Simone, Sinead, Skye, Sooz, Sophie, Stacey, Sue, Susan, Sunita, Suzie, Tamara, Teresa, Tifa, Tiffany, Toni, Tomoko, Tracey, Vanessa, Vicky, Vikki, Vicki, Wiola, Winnie, Yolanda, Yumi, Zerrin, Zoe, Zoh

And to Mathieu, who lived with this book long before anyone else had to. Merci. Jusqu'au trait.

CONTENTS

INTRODUCTION 13

HOW TO USE THIS BOOK 23
A Note on Privacy and Safety 23
What This Book Isn't 24
Final Practical Note 25

CHAPTER ONE: A CROWDED LANDSCAPE 26
Naming the Gap, Revealing the Ask 29
The Chicken-and-Egg Problem:
Breaking the Adoption Barrier 32
The Macro Lens: Why Asking Matters
Beyond the Individual 38
Micro-Level Stories: Seeing Just Ask in Action 42
The Ripple Effect: Forecasting a Just Ask Future 44
Synthesis and Forward Momentum 45

CHAPTER TWO: AT WORK, ASKING WORKS 48
How Far We've Come; How Far We Haven't 48
The Modern Confidence Gap at Work 50
Small Moments, Large Consequences 52
Global Contours: How Culture Shapes Asking 55
The Economics of Asking 57
The Mechanics of Asking: A Pragmatic Framework.....58
Five Workplace Scenarios to Think About 60

Pushback and Limits 63
Why the Workplace Matters..64
Closing: Practising in Public by Starting in Private 64

CHAPTER THREE: HEALTH, NOT HUSH 66
The Unequal Body 66
The Everyday Permission Gap in Healthcare................73
Why Asking Matters..76
The Systemic Costs of Silence...77
The AI Factor: Preparation Lowers the Barrier 79
The Mechanics of Just Ask in Healthcare......................83
Five Health-related Scenarios to Think About 86
Pushback and Limits 89
Why Health Matters 90

CHAPTER FOUR: EQUALS, NOT ECHOES 92
The New Landscape of Relationships 92
Systems in Transition 94
The Everyday Dynamics of Asking 95
Preparation as Power: Where AI Fits.............................98
When Relationships End 100
Beyond the Couple 103
The Mechanics of Just Ask in Relationships 106
Five Relationship Scenarios to Think About 109
Pushback and Limits 112
Why Relationships Matter..113

CHAPTER FIVE: FINANCE AND WEALTH - THE PRICE OF HESITATION 116

The Money Gap Nobody Talks About 116
Where Confidence Meets Consequence 118
The Systems that Profit from Silence 122
The Wealth Problem 124
Where AI Enters the Picture 126
What Changes at Scale 127
The Mechanics of Just Ask in Finance 129
Five Finance Scenarios to Think About 132
Pushback and Limits 135
Why Finance Matters 137

CHAPTER SIX: PUBLIC LIFE - ASKING FOR SPACE 139

Scene-Setting: Women Showing up in Public 139
From Frustration to Force 145
Why Women Pull Back 147
When Women Shape the Agenda 149
Where Technology Lowers Barriers 152
The Mechanics of Just Ask in Public Life 155
Five Public Life Scenarios to Think About 158
Pushback and Limits 161
Why Public Life Matters 162

CHAPTER SEVEN: THE CARE ECONOMY - CONFIDENCE IN AGEING AND SUPPORT 165

The Call Nobody's Ready For 165
Caring for Elderly Parents: Inside the Maze 169
Where Technology Can Lower the Barrier 174
The Sandwich Generation: Caring in Two Directions ... 177

Where Confidence Enters...181
Children with Complex Needs..183
The Mechanics of Just Ask in Care................................187
Five Care-Related Scenarios to Think About 193
Pushback and Limits 198
Why Care Matters 199

CHAPTER EIGHT: EYES OPEN 202
Weapons of Mass Confidence 202
Part One: The Tools Can Turn...203
Part Two: The Equity Problem We're Creating.............213
Part Three: Why We Do It Anyway 221
Closing: What to Do Tomorrow......................................224

INTRODUCTION

Every major technological leap arrives wrapped in panic. It was said that the printing press would flood the world with dangerous ideas, railways would cause women's wombs to fly out of their bodies (according to doctors no less) and the internet was going to destroy traditional education and close schools. Remember when we believed Y2K would crash global infrastructure and accidentally launch a nuclear weapon or two? There's even a name for this: the "Tech Panic Cycle", that hockey-stick graph that shows our collective fear shooting up, peaking, then gradually declining as we all get used to the thing we were convinced would kill us. We recently lived through it with social media.

Now it's artificial intelligence (AI) and specifically the consumer-facing bit: large language models (which we call LLMs) like ChatGPT, Claude and Gemini that anyone with a phone or a laptop can access. The headlines currently ping-pong between utopia and dystopia. Will these tools liberate us from drudgery, or replace us wholesale? Or both?!

For anyone new to them, LLMs are extremely sophisticated text prediction engines – tech systems trained on vast amounts of human language scraped from the internet, designed to generate text that sounds natural and informed. You type a question or prompt, and the model predicts the next most likely words in sequence, drawing on its training data (aka the internet). The output can read like it was written by a human, but the tool itself doesn't "know" anything at all in the conscious sense. It's pattern recognition at a totally monumental scale. Most publicly available tools currently have free and paid tiers, and all require an internet connection and a healthy dose of common sense. The magic lies not in the machine's intelligence, but in the quality of the questions we ask it. It's your smarts that give it the edge.

Here's what I know: AI's impact will be profound, entire industries will reshape, power structures will shift and consequences we can't predict yet will arrive, both overtly and covertly. Meanwhile, economists are now debating which jobs will vanish – and increasingly, it's a case of *when* they will vanish, not if. Regulators are scrambling to play catch-up and ethicists warn about fact and fiction blurring beyond all recognition. It's true, there will be huge winners and massive losers, and horrendous abuses will happen; we can't pretend otherwise.

We've already seen how emerging technologies can skew dark fast, and how they can spread prejudice and entrench inequality instead of adding tangible value to our lives. Misinformation already travels at the speed of send and AI makes that a thousand times faster. There's the surveillance state now emerging and the realities of diminishing privacy in our daily lives, plus the grim new era of dirty electoral tactics that AI will likely supercharge. Also there's the overwhelming issue of the concentration of power in a handful of companies with the resources to train these models, leaving both entire nations and individuals dependent on technology they don't own or control. And there's the quieter risk too: that turning to machines for every answer, from the critically important to the banal, could erode human judgement entirely and decimate our critical thinking.

And for women, some of the darkest consequences are already visible. AI-generated deepfakes are being used to humiliate and silence women, often public figures and teenage girls alike. Sexually explicit synthetic images now account for the majority of deepfake content online, according to research from Deeptrace and the BBC, and the victims are overwhelmingly female. "Sextortion" is now a thing too. It refers to the coercion of individuals, most often young women and girls, into sharing sexual images or money under threat of exposure, typically after being deceived or hacked. The rise of AI has amplified this crime, with perpetrators now using deepfake technology to fabricate explicit images from innocent photos or social media content, making it harder for victims to prove the material is fake. Law enforcement agencies, including the FBI and Europol, have warned that AI-driven sextortion is rising sharply, creating new psychological, reputational and legal harms at unprecedented scale.

Add to that the resurgence of hyper-gendered gaming cultures, the rise of AI "girlfriend" bots programmed for submission, and the quiet normalisation of digital misogyny, and you start to see a new frontier for gender inequality taking shape before our eyes. These realities sit very uneasily beside the optimism in this book, but they can't be ignored. It's the elephant in the room, for sure. The challenge is to look squarely at both: the harm and the hope, the danger and the potential.

This barely scratches the surface of the worries we all hold over the dawning of a new technological age. These risks are here now, shaping the next decade of life as we know it. I'll unpack them a bit further as we get into it. Eye contact with that elephant is essential.

But acknowledging risk isn't the same as simply surrendering to it, because alongside the dangers, AI offers us remarkable potential too, and *that's* where this book begins. I want to put that very long list of concerns aside. Not so that I ignore rather than face them, but instead to make room for something more nuanced among all the negative noise surrounding the advance of AI. Where others may see the end of a working life as we know it as robots come for our jobs, I see a female-first perspective that could be truly, mind-blowingly transformative. Adjacent to all the hype and hysteria, what I see is a vast potential upside for women, a perspective summed up with one word: confidence. Yes, it's about efficiency, but it's also about empowerment. And for women especially, I believe AI could close one of the most stubborn gaps of all: the Confidence Gap. That subtle, silent drag on female ambition, health outcomes, financial resilience and success in all its forms.

I'm talking about everyday confidence, the kind that fluctuates constantly. Yes, women are earning degrees in record numbers, founding billion-dollar companies, shaping political movements and rewriting cultural norms. Confidence has carried women into boardrooms and parliaments, and into scientific and creative industries that once shut them out. These are generational shifts, and of course I celebrate them. In fact, I count myself as a tiny data point in that mix: a woman who's launched, scaled and sold two businesses, now on to her third.

But many women are still losing out in ways that are both obvious and unseen. And not just in corporate life or in our careers – although we're still fighting for equal footing there too. I mean in our plain old average daily lives: like at the GP surgery, where symptoms get annoyingly brushed aside; in phone calls with utility companies where we're batted between departments and get nowhere; and in the legal jargon of property paperwork, where hesitation costs us thousands. And in a million other small, excruciating ways too.

We know confidence these days is about leaning in at work. But I think it's about having the self-belief to ask sharp, informed questions in *every* situation we find ourselves in, to push back when required, to negotiate in every corner of life when we're told to wait, to settle and to let it go. When we tell ourselves to just pay the inflated boiler quote for an easier bloody life.

This is where AI comes in.

Tools like ChatGPT and Claude offer something women have rarely been given: a rehearsal room. A personal space to seek vital information, draft the difficult email, practise the impossible conversation, decode jargon and try out the language of self-advocacy without fear of judgement or humiliation.

I discovered this for myself, and I now have a growing list of examples where these tools have exponentially improved the outcome of a tricky situation. I've negotiated down utility bills by sticking to a strict script, I've decoded the impossible small print of a rental contract and saved myself a decent amount of cash and I've navigated intricate eldercare policies in a country where a parent lives but I don't. Plus a hundred other small wins too ordinary to mention.

And the experience made me bolder, not just in what I asked for in the moment, but in gradually building a belief in myself that I can recreate this pattern, again and again. And if I can do this – as someone who's never overtly lacked confidence – what about the millions of women who struggle to show up for themselves with ease? How will it empower them? Now imagine what that means, not just for individual lives, but for society and the economy in broad terms.

And here's the hypothesis I can't let go of: confidence changes how women *spend*.

Do you replace the car, or put it off for another year? Will you book the long-haul trip, or leave it in the bucket list folder? Might you splash out on that insanely priced stainless-steel fridge or stick with your old poorly performing model? With a newfound confidence, would you enrol in the course, start the business, buy the laptop, do the renovation or commission the artwork? Put simply, do you hang back, wallet snapped shut, fearful of making an expensive mistake, or spend, spend, spend confidently, safe in the knowledge you got exactly what you wanted or needed at the right price?

Multiply those micro-decisions across half the global population, because women do make up half the population, whether we're visible or not, and the economic upside is potentially extraordinary. In 2015 McKinsey estimated that advancing women's equality could add $12 trillion to global GDP by 2025. While we missed that deadline, imagine the impact if millions of women suddenly had both the information they needed at their fingertips *and* the confidence to ask, push back, negotiate or simply spend money on things that previously felt out of reach. Would they spend more, and would they spend like men?

The story of AI doesn't have to be *just* about lost jobs or the end of society as we know it. It could *also* be about women winning, one contested parking ticket and one salary negotiation at a time. It's women powering up. Or at least it could be.

But there's a problem that could derail this revolution. Right now, women are adopting AI at a slower rate than men. Early surveys suggest men are more likely to experiment with LLMs, test them at work, use them for problem-solving and find smart shortcuts to get ahead. If that

Adoption Gap persists, the very tools that could close the Confidence Gap between men and women could instead widen the existing economic and professional divides. That's why this book insists on urgency, because access without uptake isn't empowerment, it's the opposite. And we can't let that happen.

I write not as an academic or an AI researcher, but as a communications professional, someone who knows both the immense power of words and the peril of a badly written press release. I have over two decades of experience in observing how language and confidence shape women's behaviour and the outcomes they live with because of that. My optimism comes from being a 40-something woman who started asking ChatGPT about care home systems and learned fast that these tools really can shift the balance in the everyday decisions that quietly shape our lives.

A note on who this book is for. The start point for my thinking and the examples I use assume a baseline of access to technology, to the internet, to the English language and to some degree of economic freedom or at least agency. This book speaks primarily to women who have resources and ideas but lack confidence to fully deploy them. The time-poor but not perhaps the income-poor. Women who can afford the car but hesitate to negotiate the finance. Who could commission the renovation but delay for fear of getting it wrong. Who have a savings pot sitting in a low-interest account because investing feels intimidating. This is not a small demographic, it represents millions of women across developed economies, but I'm well aware it's not everyone. Women without internet access, without digital literacy, or without basic economic security face different and more urgent barriers. AI won't solve structural poverty, literacy gaps, or the digital divide. The direction of travel for this book is grounded in those who have opportunity but lack confidence to seize it. That narrower mission is the focus here, because this particular gap feels both urgent and solvable.

I also need to address the trust factor.

These tools are astonishing, but still at the toddler stage of their evolution. They draw on everything the internet has ever said, which means the brilliance and the bias of the entire web come bundled together. Answers often sound more confident than they should, and on any given day the model might contradict itself completely. That's part of their charm but also their risk. The best way to use them is the same way you'd treat a colleague at work who seems bright but untested: helpful, but never the final authority. Ask for sources, cross-check against credible institutions and notice when it echoes your own assumptions or enthusiasms too neatly. This bit is particularly captivating, especially the eagerness. Neutral prompts usually get you further than loaded ones. A little rigour turns the tool from a novelty into something genuinely empowering.

AI can give you both the language and the courage to achieve a lot. What it can't give you is discernment, which is where your own judgement steps in. Think of it as a conversation between human intuition and machine efficiency. The opportunity lies in that exchange.

What follows is a map of possibility rather than a list of predictions, a way to reframe AI's arrival in our lives as something more useful and optimistic. I've kept one eye on the existential threat parked on the horizon – it's hard not to – but my priority has been to delve into the potential of a practical, sometimes playful tool for narrowing the Confidence Gap and fast-tracking women towards fairer outcomes.

This book is about the upsides of women everywhere gaining fluency in a new kind of language: the prompts, phrases and questions that unlock a whole lot of opportunity. It's about curiosity leading to capability, and capability leading to confidence. And if that starts with cancelling a pointless direct debit or finally sorting out a pension plan, then good, because small wins have a way of compounding.

The momentum around AI will continue to come at us from every direction, from governments and corporations to the technologists who build and evolve the systems. But I feel the quieter revolution may begin elsewhere: with a woman on the sofa, typing a question, reflecting on the answer and deciding to act on her expanded knowledge. Multiply that by millions, even billions, and you get something far bigger than a technological shift. You get a social one.

That's what this book is about. The potential for AI to be a *Weapon of Mass Confidence*.

HOW TO USE THIS BOOK

My goal has been to ensure this book is both useful and interesting. I know not everyone reads books cover to cover and I've tried to accommodate this. You can do that if you wish, of course. Equally you can flick straight to the chapters that interest you most.

I'm also aware that knowledge and experience with AI will vary enormously from reader to reader. Some will be huge sceptics, and because of this, have been actively rejecting it. Many are curious but are yet to have a go. Others already claim they can't live without it. And there's a huge spectrum in between. Depending on where you are with AI, some chapters will be far more compelling than others. I'm okay with that, too.

Think of this book as both a narrative and a reference tool. Read the parts that interest you right now; mentally bookmark the sections that might matter later.

A NOTE ON PRIVACY AND SAFETY

Throughout the book, I sometimes suggest uploading documents, sharing personal information and using AI for sensitive topics. *Please use private modes* where available, *do not share highly sensitive data* (medical records with identifying information, financial account numbers, etc.), and remember that anything you put into a free AI tool could theoretically be seen by others or used to train future models.

If a task involves genuinely private information, like legal documents in a contentious divorce or medical records related to a serious diagnosis, consider:

- Anonymising details before uploading (use placeholder names, remove identifying information)
- Using paid versions of tools with stronger privacy commitments
- Consulting a professional rather than relying on AI alone.

The scenarios in this book assume you're being sensible about data protection. Use your common sense.

WHAT THIS BOOK ISN'T

Let me be clear about what you won't find here:

This is not a technical guide to AI.
I won't teach you how LLMs work under the hood, how to code or how to build your own models. I'm sure there are a lot of experts on that – I'm not one of them.

This is not a comprehensive AI ethics review.
I address risks and harms, but not exhaustively. If you want deep dives into algorithmic bias or existential risk, other authors cover this better than I could.

This is not a substitute for professional advice.
AI can help you prepare for conversations with doctors, lawyers, financial advisers and therapists, but it's not a replacement for them. If you're facing serious legal trouble, a major health crisis, or a mental health emergency, *you need humans*, not chatbots.

This is not a miracle cure for inequality.
Confidence and AI won't fix patriarchy, erase the pay gap, close the Permission Gap or dismantle structural barriers in society overnight. Systemic change requires shifts that take decades. This book is about what you can do right now, in the system as it exists, while also pushing for that system to improve.

FINAL PRACTICAL NOTE

If you're genuinely new to AI tools, spend 30 minutes playing with ChatGPT, Claude or Gemini (there are free versions of each) before diving into the chapters. Ask silly questions. Ask it to plan a dream trip to a bucket list destination. Ask it to explain quantum physics like you're five. Get comfortable with the interface and the conversational flow. The number of people, especially women, I've spoken to who are vocal, angry rejectors of this tech without ever having tried it is remarkable. Give it a go.

CHAPTER ONE: A CROWDED LANDSCAPE

Walk into any airport bookshop and you'll find a wall of titles promising to make you bolder, braver and more self-assured. Because there's nothing quite like a long-haul flight to take stock of your shortcomings, right? They're written with kind and sincere intentions, often by people with lived experience of the problem, often quite brutal. They offer theories and tips, along with frameworks, rules to live by, even daily mantras to help you manifest inner bravery. In their own way, they're all pushing towards the same horizon, helping women find the confidence to step forward rather than hold back. But a lot of them stop at the individual and treat confidence as if it were an internal puzzle to be solved. As though you could just adjust your mindset, visualise success, dial up your presence and poise and lean in a little harder, and the rest would naturally follow. I subscribe to this to an extent, but not entirely.

This advice feels a bit one-dimensional to me because confidence isn't just about how you feel inside – it's also about how the world responds when you speak or act. This is the bit that rarely gets acknowledged, that confidence is inherently social and situational. It's not just about how you show up in the world, it's how the world shows up in response. It works like a currency that we're constantly trading: invisible, variable, unevenly distributed and yet hugely powerful in determining how much weight our words and actions carry. And exactly like money, you're aware when you don't have enough of it, because you can feel the deficit. In the workplace, it's watching your ideas float past unheard, only to be applauded when they're repeated by someone else. Proof that volume isn't the problem – attention around the table is. In healthcare, it's feeling your concerns minimised until a male partner steps in and repeats them. For women, I believe this gap is a construct of the system in which we live.

With three decades as an adult now under my belt, I have concluded that the world has quietly conditioned women to be cautious in how they show up and I think this is true across many cultures and in most workplaces to varying degrees. They're encouraged to think carefully about how they ask, to be deferential, even apologetic in how they push for what they want, and for generations now, confidence has been framed less as a resource to cultivate and more as a risk to manage. It's a cliché, but clichés exist for a reason: think about all the little girls who get labelled bossy, even as young as three or four. I see you.

Confidence is also in constant flux, which explains why one minute you're happily channelling your best persuasive energy to dodge a parking ticket, but the next you're feeling too awkward to send back food in a restaurant that has arrived at the table cold.

All this results in what we'll call the "Permission Gap". An unspoken but deeply embedded... well, *pause*. I suspect every woman knows exactly what I mean here. A hesitation around what women are permitted to question, express, challenge or demand. I've worked with countless wonderful women over the years who will regularly start sentences with an apology, most of the time not even noticing they do it. In all my professional career, I don't think I've heard a man do that. Not once.

I believe that hesitation carries a cost. It influences everything from pay equity to healthcare outcomes, even how mundane household responsibilities get divided between partners in some relationships. It shapes who gets heard in boardrooms and who doesn't, who leads on childcare arrangements and who doesn't, who insists on second medical opinions and who feels obliged to defer to that classic sentiment of "doctor knows best". It influences which adult sibling steps up when an elderly parent needs end-of-life support. (Sending love to the women I know, and those I don't, living through this particularly difficult chapter.)

I'm certain that the Permission Gap is an invisible yet rigid architecture that has been knocking around for generations, and one of the sizeable pillars holding up the everyday inequality that's holding women back. There are several others, but this one feels within closest reach for us, collectively as women, to start to dismantle.

So, here's my starting point for this book. Instead of treating confidence as a personality trait you either have or don't, I'm treating it as a resource that can be built and, importantly, scaled. And I'm making the case that we now have tools that can make that resource more accessible – AI, and specifically LLMs like ChatGPT, Gemini, Claude and the like. There will potentially be a few more on the scene by the time you're reading this.

They won't magically erase situational fear; we probably need some sort of chip implant in our brains for that. But right now these tools can act as laser-sharp information gatherers, fantastic rehearsal partners, thought organisers and language refiners. They help us prepare for the nightmare conversation before we have it, they give us words in situations where we know we might struggle and they let us practise the ask, whatever it is, until it feels natural. I will unpack exactly *how* in the chapters to follow, but I deeply believe for many women that tiny shift, just having a structured way to research and prepare, has the potential to be transformative.

This leads to the bigger "what if?" question I also keep coming back to: what happens if millions of women start asking LLMs more questions, and in turn, begin asking for more in life generally? That feels like an exciting, gendered upside to AI.

NAMING THE GAP, REVEALING THE ASK

We spend a lot of time mentally rehearsing scenarios that impact our lives, from the irritating to the catastrophic. Research by NatCen Social Research in 2023 found that women are significantly more likely than men to report high levels of worry across personal, financial and professional domains, something we're told grew in and then persisted after the Covid-19 pandemic. In the workplace the internal loop often plays out like this: *What if I push too hard and it backfires? What if I look naïve? What if I say the wrong thing? What if the answer is no? What if I embarrass myself?* These "what ifs" blow up in our minds until they're exaggerated, increasing the likelihood of the question never leaving our lips at all.

But what if we asked anyway?

The important "what if" should be: what if it worked? What if the redundancy package came back higher because you put a bulletproof rationale together? What if the solicitor slowed down and explained the contract line by line because you refused to nod along in silence? What if you challenged the bank's first mortgage offer and spotted an adjustment that saved you thousands? What if asking clearly, calmly, without a hint of apology was the hinge between loss and opportunity?

The truth is that in so many of life's critical moments, for women silence is more expensive than speaking. It literally costs us more, whether that's in time or money, or even just emotional energy, which we will always eventually run out of, despite having deep reserves. Yet for so many women, silence feels that bit safer and compliance seems to preserve relationships. We've learned that swallowing questions often avoids humiliation or awkward situations. The cost of that conditioning is far beyond theoretical, it's financial and also deeply personal. It shows up in the missed salary review, the health insurance wrangling that felt too hard, the visa application that defeated you with bureaucracy and the landlord dispute that created months of stress.

This is where *Just Ask* comes in – what if you *Just Ask*?

Two little words that shift the burden and become an inner prompt of sorts, and I'll say this now, I'm going to use these two words a lot. Not in a cringy slogan kind of way, more as a practical recalibration. Instead of carrying the entire labyrinth of options in your head, along with the doubts and the worst-case scenarios, you simply externalise it. You Just Ask. You harness modern technology to push for clarity and then you put the weight back where it belongs: on the system, the institution, or just the person on the other end of the phone, saying no when you think it could be yes.

AI changes the stakes around this dynamic dramatically.

For the first time, women can rehearse not only the words but the consequences too. You can simulate the intricacies of a negotiation with a machine that roleplays your manager, your lawyer, your financial adviser, your kid's teacher, your in-laws or even your difficult neighbour. You can anticipate the "no" and practise the follow-up until it lands. You can walk into once-intimidating conversations already armed with language and logic.

It can be a small, convenient life upgrade and it also has the potential to be an equaliser. Using Just Ask as an inner motivator is essentially about recognising that silence has a cost. TO YOU! And across a lifetime these costs accumulate, they shrink choices, dim ambitions, limit potential, erode security and they'll all probably live in your mind rent-free for decades as regrets.

Clearly asking is not a guarantee of getting what you want – let's not lose sight of reality here. But it's a damn good way of refusing invisibility. And when enough women adopt this shift, the knock-on effects move far beyond the individual. At scale, I hold the view they'll recalibrate what institutions expect and eventually how markets respond. That's the bigger, more ambitious story this book sets out to tell. Yes, it's about highlighting the potential for every woman to start nailing and cataloguing small wins, but more importantly, it's about putting forward a compelling case for how the simple act of asking great bloody questions could reshape women's economic and social standing over time. Because what if the only thing standing between where we are and where we could be is that default habit of silence that's annoyingly ingrained into so many of us?

THE CHICKEN-AND-EGG PROBLEM: BREAKING THE ADOPTION BARRIER

Before we go further, I need to acknowledge another elephant in the room, or perhaps more accurately, the chunky paradox at the heart of this entire book that I can already hear critics calling out.

If lack of confidence is the problem, and AI tools are the solution, there's an uncomfortable circular logic at play: these tools require confidence to adopt in the first place.

The women who most need them, those overwhelmed by complexity or uncertainty, or time-poor from juggling multiple responsibilities, are precisely the ones least likely to experiment with new technology. Meanwhile, men who already possess baseline confidence are racing ahead.

The data bears this out uncomfortably. Pew Research Center found in 2024 that men were 40% more likely than women to have used AI tools like ChatGPT for work-related tasks. McKinsey's 2025 survey across multiple countries showed women were less likely to experiment with AI, less likely to use it for problem-solving, and far less likely to feel confident in its output. We're watching a Confidence Gap create an Adoption Gap, which then widens the original Confidence Gap. It's a vicious cycle.

So how do we break it?

The answer lies in understanding how technology adoption actually spreads, not through overnight conversion, but through gradual diffusion. Sociologist Everett Rogers spent decades studying how innovations move through populations, and his findings are instructive here. Adoption doesn't happen all at once. It starts with a small group of "innovators" (roughly 2.5% of any population) who experiment fearlessly with new tools simply because they're new. Then come the "early adopters" (13.5%), who are more pragmatic: they see strategic value and dive in despite imperfections.

Only after these early cohorts prove a technology's value does the "early majority" (34%) begin to engage. These are the pragmatists, the wait-and-see crowd, the women who've been burned before by overhyped solutions. They need proof, not promises. They need to see their peers succeeding, they're not interested in hearing tech evangelists harking on.

This is where we are right now with AI and women. The innovators and early adopters, skewing male, are already fluent. The early majority, where most women sit, are watching, waiting, and millions are wondering if it's worth the effort.

Here's the crucial insight: the early majority don't need to become nerdy technologists. They simply need three things:

- **Permission from trusted sources**
  Women are more likely to adopt new tools when recommended by people they trust – family, friends, colleagues and mentors. This is why representation matters. When a woman sees another woman, particularly one who shares her circumstances, using AI to solve a problem she recognises, adoption becomes far more imaginable. This book aims to be one of those trusted sources, offering honest assessment of where these tools help and where they don't.

- **Low-stakes entry points**
  The biggest barrier to adoption is fear of looking foolish or wasting precious time. Here's the thing – women don't need to "master AI", they just need

one small, successful interaction that proves it can add value and is worth the effort. That might be asking ChatGPT to summarise a dense policy document, or using it to draft a tricky email, or getting it to decode changes in tax law or benefits eligibility. Or it could be using it to identify every cake shop in walkable distance from a station on a day trip. No judgement here. One win creates curiosity. Curiosity prompts you to ask again.

- **Community and shared learning**
  By and large, women are natural collaborators. When adoption happens in clusters – colleagues showing colleagues, friends sharing prompts in group chats, daughters walking their mum through how to use these tools – confidence spreads more virally. This is already happening in pockets. In online communities, women are trading AI "recipes" for everything from preparing job applications to drafting menu plans for picky eaters, to researching startup investment strategies. The more these practices are normalised, the faster hesitation falls away.

The adoption curve for women and AI is following the same pattern we've seen documented with other transformative technologies. Remember when online banking felt risky and complicated? Women initially adopted it a lot more slowly than men, citing security concerns and preference for in-person service. But once a critical mass engaged, once friends confirmed it was safe, once the saved time and convenience became undeniable, adoption accelerated rapidly. By 2020, UK Finance reported that women and men used online banking at near-equal rates.

Mobile technology followed a similar trajectory. You may remember that early phones (including car phones!) were marketed to businessmen. Women were slower to adopt, often keeping simpler "analogue phones" longer. But when smartphones proved essential for managing family logistics, coordinating care and staying connected with friends and family, women didn't just catch up, they became the power users. Today, women spend more time on smartphones than men across nearly every age group.

What do I take away from this? That women's slower initial adoption of technology often reflects rational and justifiable caution. When the value becomes clear and the friction falls away, women don't just participate, they often lead.

AI is at that inflection point right now. The tools are gradually moving from experimental to essential. The women who engage today won't just benefit individually, they'll become the bridges that bring millions more along with them. I've been on a one-woman mission to convert women in recent months. I've lost count of the times I've sat down for coffee or lunch with a friend and insisted on a quick tutorial, which more often than not blew their minds.

If you're reading this and thinking, *"This sounds interesting, but I'm not a tech person,"* I have two responses.

First: you don't need to be. The tools I'm describing require no coding, no technical knowledge, no special expertise. If you can use Google, you can use ChatGPT. If you've ever sent an email, you can prompt an AI. The barrier is psychological, not technical, I promise.

Second: your hesitation is *the point*. The fact that you're uncertain, that you're weighing whether this is worth your limited time and energy, that you're wondering if it's overhyped... that's exactly why you need to experiment. Because the alternative isn't neutrality. It's falling further behind in systems increasingly shaped by people who aren't hesitating.

The women currently using AI at scale aren't smarter than you, more capable than you or more deserving of advantage in life. They just started six months earlier. And six months of fluency compounds into measurable advantages in today's world – in salary negotiation and healthcare advocacy, in financial decision-making and researching how and where to spend your hard-earned money.

Here's the uncomfortable truth: the Confidence Gap won't close itself, and AI won't sit politely on the sidelines waiting for women to feel ready. The gap is widening right now, today, in real time. Every day you delay experimenting is another day someone else gets better at using these tools and you don't.

But here's the hopeful reality: you don't need to close the entire gap tomorrow. You just need to take one small step today. Open ChatGPT and ask it a question you've been avoiding researching. Use it to draft an email you've been putting off. Feed it a document you don't understand and ask it to reduce it to simple bullet points.

One interaction. That's the ask.

Because confidence, like adoption, compounds. The woman who successfully uses AI once is exponentially more likely to use it again. The woman who uses it twice starts to see patterns in where it helps. The woman who uses it ten times begins to develop fluency. And the woman who uses it 50 times? She's not thinking about whether to adopt any more. She's thinking about what to ask next, as she eats the meal ChatGPT encouraged her to cook. A meal made up of the random assortment of food in her fridge on the brink of expiry that she was reluctantly going to throw out, until she casually typed in a prompt and got handed a perfect recipe.

This book exists to compress that learning curve, to give you the 50 interactions' worth of insight up front, so your first experiment doesn't feel like a leap into the void but a step onto solid ground.

THE MACRO LENS: WHY ASKING MATTERS BEYOND THE INDIVIDUAL

Let's get into the big-picture piece – I hold the view that the Permission Gap is a societal issue versus an individual problem, and that its impact cascades outward, subtly shaping the world's economies and the institutions that run them. It underpins the social norms we're all now so familiar with as women, and we're well and truly conditioned to adhere to those behavioural models.

Now that an obsession with data is firmly embedded in our society, both personal and collective, the consequences of women under-asking are to an extent measurable. In global workplaces, a 2018 *Harvard Business Review* study found that women who asked for a pay rise secured one only 15% of the time, compared with 20% for men, underscoring how "under-asking" directly depresses earnings. Multiply those small gaps across decades and across millions of workers and the loss gets to remarkable proportions pretty quickly, not just in wages but in accrued pensions, bonuses, promotions and payouts. Every conversation avoided or under-delivered compounds into that structural shortfall.

This then pushes my mind in the direction of entrepreneurship, an area that tells a more complex story when you dig around. Yes, women are founding companies in growing numbers, and many have scaled them extremely successfully – think Canva, Bumble, 23andMe, Glossier and StitchFix. But female-founded startups still receive a disproportionately small share of venture capital, even when performance metrics are equal or superior. According to PitchBook's 2024 *All In* report, companies with at least one female founder raised $38.8 billion in 2024, an increase in dollar volume, but their share of total capital and deal dominance actually shrank. Ouch.

That disparity has several roots – the bias of investors, access to networks, institutional inertia and old-fashioned structural constraints – but confidence, and how to frame a compelling, even aggressive funding ask, has to be a contributing factor.

A 2018 Harvard Business School working paper found that male entrepreneurs are more likely to *over*estimate their valuation and future growth, which leads them to ask for larger rounds. This behaviour gets rewarded in the gilet-wearing venture capitalist world. Meanwhile, many female founders report adjusting their ask downward to avoid being labelled "greedy" or "ambitious". (If you want a deeper dive into the psychology behind this, the HBS working paper *Overconfidence and Entrepreneurial Investment* by Ulrike Malmendier and Geoffrey Tate is worth a look.)

It would be an untrue generalisation to imply that women in business lack confidence broadly, but it's true that, in the hyper-competitive arena of venture investing, a small hesitation in asking big can inadvertently become a large funding difference. Each time a pitch is downsized or declined, it's a personal setback. It could also be a groundbreaking or life-saving innovation that never sees the light of day, despite it having huge potential to benefit society as a whole. Or it could mean a founder who never scales to fulfil the true potential of the business.

The field of healthcare reveals a particularly fascinating picture too when we view it through the lens of the Confidence Gap, and it's an area that I feel gets limited airtime. Women's symptoms are more likely to be misdiagnosed or dismissed, a depressing phenomenon documented in studies from Stanford and the *British Medical Journal*, plus many more. Women frequently under-ask for second opinions and often struggle to self-advocate effectively, with consequences ranging from delayed treatment to preventable pain and suffering. I firmly maintain that under-asking is mostly the product of systemic messaging that discourages assertiveness from women when engaging with professionals and authority figures from an unfamiliar world, and in every arena – financial, legal, professional, health – the expected habit of silence or deference ultimately becomes an invisible tax on opportunity.

And then there's culture and society more broadly. Nations that actively promote gender equality and women's participation in public life (shout out to the Nordic countries) consistently show higher rates of female labour-force participation, entrepreneurship and innovation output. According to the World Economic Forum's *Global Gender Gap Report 2024*, Iceland, Norway and Finland all continue to lead globally in gender parity, and the OECD links this progress directly to inclusive policy design and cultural norms that support women's agency and assertiveness in decision-making. Meanwhile, in regions where social norms still discourage women from speaking up or managing household finances, the World Bank's *Women, Business and the Law 2024* index records lower female workforce participation and slower economic growth. A comprehensive cultural comparison of assertiveness norms has yet to be undertaken as far as I know, but lived experience and the data we do have point in the same direction: where women are encouraged to act and ask, economies tend to move faster.

AI lands in a world already shaped by those uneven realities, one where women's voices are still filtered through bias, but where the tools for helping us redress that imbalance have finally arrived. That's what makes this moment so interesting. LLMs can't single-handedly rewrite generations of conditioning, but they can close some of the practical gaps it created: the gaps in knowledge, access, preparation and confidence. They give women faster ways to find information, rehearse difficult conversations and decode bureaucratic systems that once demanded expertise or social capital to navigate. In cultures that have historically rewarded silence or deference, it's not hard to imagine that kind of access having the potential to be transformational, as AI can start to rebalance exactly who feels equipped to ask. And when the ability to ask scales, so does everything that follows: confidence and participation, and the economic upside that comes with both.

MICRO-LEVEL STORIES: SEEING *JUST ASK* IN ACTION

It's one thing to talk about macroeconomic consequences, and admittedly I'm a curious observer not an expert, and another to consider them in our day-to-day lives. But think about the woman negotiating a redundancy package – she might know her worth but freezes at the email drafting stage, worried about being perceived as money hungry. The act of asking, when you're fully informed, rehearsed and clear on the desired optimal outcome, turns what might have been a standard payout into a substantially improved package... making the economic effect immediate and tangible.

Or consider the property settlement after a parent dies and the associated bureaucracy people suddenly find themselves unwillingly thrown into. Probate documents and inheritance tax demands, heavy with legal jargon and time-sensitive clauses, can intimidate even the most capable person, and women who hesitate to question terms or demand clarifications may risk unnecessary financial loss or added complexities. Asking, backed by preparation and knowledge, can convert confusion into advantage, even if that advantage is just less stress and anxiety at a time of immense grief.

Healthcare offers parallel micro-victories too. Think of a patient who presses for more information or a second opinion who uncovers errors, miscommunication or even a misdiagnosis. For most people, I suspect it's rarely that dramatic. Instead they're quiet, everyday interventions that accumulate one by one into improved long-term well-being. And they're also representative of a broader truth: asking good questions is fundamentally about accessing digestible information and then finding the motivation to act on it.

Even workplace visibility can be shaped by small, decisive asks, from being prepared for the annual review to requesting a mentor or pitching for project leadership. A simple "can I contribute here?" often unlocks opportunities that remain invisible until someone claims them. Now, for the first time, women can rehearse and refine these asks with AI, putting their case together, simulating manager responses, generating persuasive phrasing, building data-backed arguments and anticipating objections. The combination of preparation using AI and boldness from being aware of the Confidence Gap converts potential hesitancy into meaningful leverage. At least, that's the potential and the hope!

THE RIPPLE EFFECT: FORECASTING A *JUST ASK* FUTURE

Now let's scale these examples.

Imagine millions of women thinking "what if I just ask?" in their workplaces, in their homes, in GP surgeries and in every part of society they encounter. Not as a cringy mantra or an ideal, but simply as a repeatable, practical habit. If women asked more and negotiated more, what might happen?

Economically, the effects surely would be immediate. Increased salaries compound into larger pensions and greater spending power, along with higher investment in businesses and communities. Societally, amplified voices shift traditional norms, eventually making assertive enquiry less extraordinary and more commonplace. Power balances in organisations recalibrate when women routinely show up asking the right questions, challenging assumptions, tabling better solutions and delivering better outcomes. How could they not, frankly?

Markets respond when they see clarity and demand. AI gives women the tools to generate both, by making preparation straightforward and removing the expert gatekeepers. The effect? The Confidence Gap shifts from an abstract problem to something women can actually close, one informed ask at a time.

There's a geopolitical lens to consider too – in big organisations where women collectively ask for parity, from global nonprofits to multinational corporations, policy and practice evolve, salary bands adjust and project allocations become more equitable. Leadership pipelines shift and expand to include more women, more of the time. Individually, small asks gradually push towards meaningful systemic change. When women routinely think "let me just ask" across all sectors and areas of life, the aggregate outcome is potentially tremendous; opportunity, wealth, influence and simple contentment are distributed more evenly.

Let's not get swept away with thoughts of a perfect future lurking right around the corner, however. There will always be pushback and frustrating outcomes, and women will still encounter horrendous bosses of all genders and impossible situations. Not every question has an actionable answer or clearly definable solution either. But the principle is clear: habitual asking, supported by superior intelligence and preparation, can instil levels of confidence that shift trajectories in ways that are both quantifiable and culturally transformative – and also in ways that could just make a crappy day slightly more bearable.

SYNTHESIS AND FORWARD MOMENTUM

You're now getting a sense of what I want to unpack a lot further, the definite, exciting momentum around what happens when AI and a "fuck it, what if I just ask?" mindset collide at scale. It ladders up to a future where technology doesn't replace human confidence, but amplifies it. Or at least I hope that's how my fellow optimists will see it.

Confidence, when viewed as a resource rather than a trait, is without doubt totally scalable, and giving yourself the permission to Just Ask is the lever. It transforms uncertainty into clarity and subsequent hesitation into action, meaning that a million individual opportunities can, over time, build into far greater societal impact.

The blending of AI and human judgement multiplies everyone's potential, but especially women's. Rehearsal with LLMs can turn unknown scenarios into familiar, less intimidating ones, complex negotiations get simulated and scrutinised from every possible angle and robust preparation replaces stomach-churning fear of the unknown. LLMs offer us a tool that is both methodical and repeatable. Just imagine their impact when it's also universally accessible.

So the question now is: where and how are you going to show up, prepped and ready to ask?

There are so many areas of life where women can and should be asking for more and pushing for more, where the Just Ask principle can be practised and mastered. Each one shows how a single habit, scaled across millions, has the power to open doors to new opportunities and optimised outcomes. The one aspect of the AI revolution we can celebrate is quiet and deliberate. It will accumulate over time and it begins with an inkling and an instinct, before it moves into an email, a phone call or a question asked aloud.

It starts with a single nudge to yourself... Just Ask.

CHAPTER TWO: AT WORK, ASKING WORKS

HOW FAR WE'VE COME; HOW FAR WE HAVEN'T

In a single working lifetime, the landscape for women has thankfully changed a lot.

Fifty years ago, office structures were rigid and hierarchical, pay disparities went unquestioned and sexual harassment didn't even have a name, it was just "a bit of harmless fun" (it's neither harmless nor fun). Women played their part in professional worlds, but more often than not in support roles as secretaries, receptionists and assistants. My mum held all three of those roles at once. The idea of a female CEO or policymaker was pretty inconceivable. Today, on paper at least, the story looks different. Women occupy leadership roles everywhere, from central banks to tech startups, and the pay gap has narrowed to an extent. Flexible work has become mainstream in recent years, though the jury's still out on whether it's here to stay.

Yet beneath these positive headlines lies a lingering and individual barrier: hesitation. Something I've felt myself on the odd occasion and noted in others over my career. It's a subject that's had a lot of airtime among friends as they critique their professional progress and wrestle with all the feelings that sit quietly alongside personal ambition.

It's the quiet second-guessing and the quick internal calculation of risk, the weighing up of consequences before making an observation or asking a question – *this* is the Permission Gap in action. The workplace has always been designed to reward asking, but historically, men have been the ones expected to ask and women have generally had to learn to navigate this world by hedging their bets and underplaying their hands. The little voice inside you calculating whether your next contribution is in some weird way… permissible.

Let me be clear on what I mean by hesitation, because I'm not talking about the odd bout of nerves. It's a more persistent behaviour many women seem to default to, the tendency to under-ask or underplay achievement. It's the instinct to delay a negotiation until the timing feels perfect or avoid a conversation entirely because the possible fallout feels too costly. And over time, these quiet choices tally into lost salary and wasted opportunity. They stall promotions and compromise influence in one of the places where it matters most. These behavioural patterns are shaped by the culture we operate in and the expectations it places on women, versus a failure in competence.

The question is, what we do about it?

I'm keen to argue two main points. First, that asking good questions works and can lead to far better outcomes than we imagine; and second, that modern tools can make asking these questions less risky, less scary and far more precise – and crucially, very repeatable. The combination of technique and technology now at our fingertips offers a practical way out of a deep-rooted behaviour that's cost women too much for too long.

THE MODERN CONFIDENCE GAP AT WORK

The data on who speaks up, who leads, who negotiates and who gets named for stretch roles won't surprise you. Across industries, and I'm sure continents too, men still dominate these spaces. A 2023 McKinsey and LeanIn.Org study found that for every 100 men promoted to a managerial role, only 87 women are, and just 82 women of colour. The gap widens with seniority: women hold only 28% of C-suite roles globally, despite entering the workforce at near-equal rates.

Women also negotiate less often and with smaller gains. Research from Harvard Kennedy School found that while 57% of men negotiate their starting salary, only 7% of women do, and even when they ask, they tend to request 20% less on average. The issue is professional culture. Women's assertiveness is still misread as aggression in many workplaces, a bias that quietly limits, even punishes, ambition.

Studies from Catalyst and *Harvard Business Review* show women are interrupted in meetings far more frequently than men and are less likely to be credited for team ideas, highlighting that visibility is another significant issue in the workplace. The same dynamic can be found everywhere, from small creative studios to multinational boardrooms. I've seen it play out across both the hemispheres I've worked in, in Sydney and in London, where the gender balance on paper looked progressive, but the confidence inside the meeting room still tilted male.

But what really matters is how all this adds up. Let's call it the "arithmetic of accumulation". (Can you tell that I'm forever wired to think in headlines?)

A single missed opportunity in year one is a kick-yourself annoyance, but ten such moments over an entire career? Quite another. Compounding a slightly lower annual raise, accepting a less prominent project, staying with a company when it's time to move on and taking a career break without adjusting financial plans lead to significant long-term effects. A woman who declines a stretch role that carries a promotion two years later might never catch up to the peer who rolled the dice and took the risk. I should mention here the now infamous study (among professional women at least) from HP which revealed that women will only apply for roles when they feel they fit 100% of the criteria, whereas men feel that ticking 60% of the requirements is sufficient to apply.

The irony, in a business world obsessed with growth, is that organisations actually miss out when they tolerate patterns of under-asking from their employees; teams lose on accelerated outcomes when they hold back from asking for more resources, and projects receive suboptimal leadership because the people best suited haven't felt able to put their hand up. And the culture becomes self-reinforcing. The loudest voices are disproportionately amplified, while the quieter, methodical ones become increasingly invisible or slip into being considered "the safe pair of hands" who gets overlooked for anything more.

Anyone who's notched a few years professionally will know that the workplace tends not to be neutral. It's been coded, to some extent unconsciously, to reward visible assertion and a subtle, culturally gendered way of working. Men and women face the same structures, but societal expectation teaches us different default behaviours. That's what the Permission Gap describes, a learned hesitation that often operates just beneath our conscious awareness.

And you might do it without ever spotting it, you're that conditioned.

SMALL MOMENTS, LARGE CONSEQUENCES

Let's consider a couple of familiar scenarios, small as individual moments, but far more consequential when multiplied:

- **The early career move**. A junior account manager receives a job offer in a company she likes and wants to accept the role. The salary is modest, in fact, the same as her current role. She hesitates, she imagines the conversation where she asks for more and is flatly told no, and so she accepts. Two years later she learns a peer who started on the same day negotiated a higher package. The difference in confidence at that critical moment created a wage divergence she'll potentially be playing catch-up on for years.

- **Project planning.** A female project lead prepares to ask for a realistic headcount allocation to deliver a complex campaign. She notes the extra work and the risk to already pressurised timelines, but imagines the budget meeting where her request for increased staff will likely be met with scepticism, so she trims the request to make it more palatable to the bosses. The project succeeds, but with extra stress and longer hours for all involved, and this compromise becomes the new normal.

Both moments could have different outcomes if the person involved had a reliable way to practise, to test language, to anticipate pushback and to rehearse responses. That practical rehearsal is where LLMs, combined with the little inner voice telling you to Just Ask, can offer tangible value.

Let's explore a few more examples. Each scenario shows how preparation and rehearsal can transform high-stakes workplace moments. Sometimes it takes an okay outcome to a greatly improved one. Other times, it's a total game changer.

- **The procurement lead.** A procurement manager for a global telecommunications firm was asked to manage a new vendor relationship covering several countries. She knew the markets, understood the compliance issues and could see the risks the business didn't yet fully appreciate. The problem was local. The senior leaders in some countries expected a deferential approach to authority that discouraged direct challenge. She used an LLM to rehearse phrasing for important stakeholder conversations. She trained the model on cultural briefing notes and anonymised past emails and then roleplayed the meeting until her responses flowed naturally. The result was precise, well-delivered, culturally sensitive and effective. Contracts were renegotiated and the organisation avoided significant cost exposure.

- **The founder on funding.** A startup founder in fintech prepared to pitch to a panel of investors known for blunt questions. Rather than improvising, as many founders tend to do, she used AI to refine her answers and tackle potential scepticism. The practice didn't remove the tough questions but it did reduce the shock factor, allowing her to stay focused and strategic when the panel pushed hard to identify cracks in her vision. She left with an offer and investor terms that respected both the venture's potential and her confidence to handle herself under tough scrutiny.

- **The senior exec and the redundancy negotiation.** A director facing redundancy prepared a data-led case to argue for an enhanced severance package. She fed project outcomes, client retention figures and the measurable impact of her work into an LLM, which produced a succinct narrative connecting her contribution over several years to the compensation on the table. She presented the case with calm evidence rather than pleading emotionally. The outcome was an improved package and an exit that allowed for a strategic career pivot, rather than a mad scramble to replace her income to pay immediate bills.

These examples are practical, repeatable interventions that convert uncertainty into empowered conversation. Remember, the point of rehearsal isn't to generate a script to recite like a robot, it's a private practice room that helps the speaker find their natural voice and sharpen arguments.

GLOBAL CONTOURS: HOW CULTURE SHAPES ASKING

The Confidence Gap plays out differently around the world and while I skew quite UK-centric with my experience and observations, it's interesting to lift the lid on it more broadly.

In some Nordic countries, norms encourage egalitarian participation, and formal structures actually exist to compensate for individual hesitation. In many parts of Asia, hierarchical business cultures reward deference and penalise direct challenge. In markets across Africa and Latin America, the interplay of gender norms and local customs produces highly distinctive patterns. Ultimately, it's about what behaviour is socially safe versus talent or capability.

These international variations are worth mentioning for two reasons.

Firstly, women who operate across borders must navigate a mosaic of expectations that differ with the time zone; and secondly, global organisations competing in diverse markets benefit when their leaders can adapt communication styles to suit local norms without losing conviction. AI-assisted rehearsal allows that adaptation because it helps a leader switch registers appropriately, becoming more direct in one context and more tempered in another, all while keeping the core argument intact.

In my early twenties, still fresh into my career, I handled the public relations for an iconic Japanese gaming company. I had to learn the nuances of interacting with executives from a very different professional culture, and do so completely on the fly. So much of it was guesswork on my part, which was intimidating, especially when I was desperate to impress. That just wouldn't be the case now.

There's also a policy angle to consider. Countries that invest in transparent pay practices, accessible childcare and supportive parental leave policies tend to create environments where asking simply feels a bit less risky. So structural reforms really do matter, but of course they take time, so tools that help individuals prepare, practise and ask the right questions create an immediate option in the meantime. LLMs are a lever that helps to accelerate women towards greater individual empowerment while we hustle our way collectively towards systemic change.

THE ECONOMICS OF ASKING

There's a persuasive financial argument for encouraging more asking too. When more women land better initial salaries and negotiate better terms, they secure more leadership roles and launch more businesses. The knock-on economic effect has the potential to be considerable.

In my experience, women tend to negotiate quite differently to men, and often for different things. But the behaviour of outcome-oriented asking repeated by millions of women compounds into measurable impact. Companies that foster cultures where asking is normal will have more diverse leadership teams and far greater retention as a result and they'll benefit from more perspectives around the table and better, faster problem-solving. So it's fair to say that the argument for encouraging asking at scale is both moral and pragmatic.

THE MECHANICS OF ASKING: A PRAGMATIC FRAMEWORK

If asking works and the stakes are high, the practical question becomes: how? The Just Ask method is straightforward.

- **Map the terrain.** Before you ask, understand the context. What are the organisational priorities? Who makes the decision and what are their likely objections? AI can scan meeting notes, organisational structures, policy documents and past decisions to paint a quick map.

- **Frame the value.** Anchor your ask in the benefit it brings the organisation. Use clear metrics where possible. Numbers aren't the only tool for persuasion, but they're persuasive levers in nearly any important ask at work.

- **Rehearse.** Practise the key lines, roleplay likely pushback and run through calm, evidence-led responses. This is where LLMs are particularly useful. They can simulate difficult personality types and present varied responses to suit the specific stakeholders you'll be dealing with.

- **Structure the ask.** Keep it crisp. Lead with the outcome you want, followed by the evidence and then a proposed next step. It reduces the chance of the conversation devolving into a debate or free-for-all.

- **Iterate.** After the conversation, reflect and refine. What worked? What surprised you? What curveballs came your way? Use the notes to improve the next rehearsal. Pop how it went into your LLM conversation while it's still fresh.

- **Scale influence.** Share successful experiences with your peers internally. When multiple people in a team adopt these habits, the organisational norm shifts from deferential silence to constructive enquiry. Also, share tips and learnings with your mates outside of work, especially those on similar journeys professionally.

These are practical moves anyone can adopt. They work best when rehearsed, because practice reduces brain strain in the moment and keeps the conversation strategic rather than impulsive or reactive.

FIVE WORKPLACE SCENARIOS TO THINK ABOUT

Theory is helpful, but understanding the practicalities of how and where to experiment might be more useful. Here are five practical ideas that synthesise these mechanics, each illustrated with a short scenario so you can see how it works in practice.

1. THE MEETING MIC

Scenario: A marketing lead uses her LLM to generate three short, high-impact contributions for a weekly steering group meeting that she sometimes struggles to contribute to. She goes in armed with a concise question, an insight grounded in data and a constructive challenge with a potential solution. In a meeting often derailed by conflicting priorities or detail, she uses one of the lines and redirects the conversation back on course. Her visibility rises routinely and she consistently participates.

How to use it: Before a meeting, ask the model for one question, one insight and one challenge relevant to the agenda. Keep them up your sleeve for use as needed. Remember, nobody should be in a meeting if they don't contribute! All bosses know this. Participation is important for a variety of reasons, and optics is one of them.

2. THE BOSS SIMULATOR

Scenario: A senior product manager is anxious about asking her director for a bigger budget. She trains a model on her director's (anonymised) emails and recent feedback, then runs a mock meeting. The model pushes back in the voice she expected. When the real meeting arrives, she's already practised the precise reframing that converts the resistance into a mutually workable compromise. Budget secured.

How to use it: Feed anonymised emails or meeting transcripts into a private model. Roleplay the conversation until your responses are crisp. Is it slightly creepy to use AI to simulate your boss and their strategies? Probably a bit, yes. But could it be extraordinarily helpful with tricky characters or in high-stakes scenarios? Absolutely.

3. THE SALARY BENCHMARK

Scenario: A project leader preparing to ask for a raise in her annual review uses AI to compile industry-specific pay data from public sources and third-party sector reports, and then builds in internal pay band info. The model produces a compelling one-page evidence sheet plus suggested phrasing. The negotiation meeting that follows feels factual and calm. She leaves with the raise she'd hoped for.

How to use it: Ask the model to triangulate salary ranges, frame comparative performance and draft a concise script that covers every likely pushback. Keep in mind that employers in these situations respond to evidence grounded in the *value* you contribute and the *costs* they'd face to replace you.

4. THE JARGON-TO-PLAIN-ENGLISH TRANSLATOR

Scenario: A campaign director receives a 30-page vendor contract full of complex legal terms and some unusual caveats. Instead of staring at it, she uploads it into an LLM and asks for a simple summary outlining the top five risk points and suggested negotiation lines. The contract is clarified in minutes, not days.

How to use it: When documents arrive, use a private LLM to summarise, identify red flags and suggest priority areas for follow-up. Prompt them to dig out the clauses that appear to be purposely hidden or unnecessarily obtuse. There's no need to feel overwhelmed by these tactics any more.

5. THE CONFIDENCE DIARY

Scenario: After every weekly CEO one-to-one, an ambitious business director enters notes into a private model and asks it to synthesise what landed well and what could be sharpened. Over several months, she builds a personalised playbook of language and evidence that boosts her confidence and makes both the one-to-ones and higher-stakes performance reviews easier to navigate.

How to use it: Keep a simple running log of conversations. Use the model to distil lessons and turn them into repeatable phrasing. We know that these tools have a bias for enthusiasm and optimism, in small doses (!), so use this to your advantage.

Each of these scenarios offers a small suggestion of ways to use LLMs as a confidence booster at work. Each is repeatable and their power is cumulative. Done well over time, they contribute to changing a culture of defaulting to silence into a culture of strategic, informed asking.

PUSHBACK AND LIMITS

Needless to say, none of this is a silver bullet; we can't lose sight of the fact that there will always be legitimate critiques and differing opinions on performance. And difficult and irrational bosses, and fuck-ups you need to own! Remember too, that AI can reflect your own biases right back at you, so it's worth keeping a tight grip on objectivity, which can be harder than it sounds. Training a model to be your biggest cheerleader without grounding it in reality might be an ego boost but it won't serve you well long term. LLMs can also suggest phrasing that sounds overly polished or unnatural, and rehearsing yourself to death for a specific meeting can make you come across as mechanical rather than credible.

And while confidence matters, some institutions are constrained by formal processes you can't simply talk your way through, like public sector organisations bound by civil service rules or regulated professions like law or medicine, even companies listed on stock exchanges with strict governance protocols. The art is knowing when to push, when to prepare, and when to sit tight because you're clued up enough to know that procedure simply has to take its course.

The pragmatist's response is to treat LLMs and rehearsal as part of a broader toolkit. They can complement the invaluable contribution mentors and networks can make. They sit alongside the policy shifts you encounter. But they really do make certain kinds of practice easier and they reduce the friction of asking.

WHY THE WORKPLACE MATTERS

The workplace felt like a natural starting point for the wider hypothesis of this book because it's where money is allocated and careers are shaped. It's where anxiety often manifests and where the rules about who speaks and who is heard are covertly designed and enforced. I believe that if asking becomes more common and less risky at work, it will show up everywhere, from individual pay packets to leadership representation, from one-off project outcomes to overall business success. Getting it right in the workplace matters so deeply because work still structures and governs so much of our adult lives.

CLOSING: PRACTISING IN PUBLIC BY STARTING IN PRIVATE

The kind of change we're chasing will arrive very gradually, as a set of repeated, private practices that alter public norms over time. And that's what asking ultimately does. It begins as an awkward sentence practised privately or as a roleplay conversation with a machine. It becomes a confident request that goes well, and then eventually it becomes ordinary. Just one more thing we do day to day.

The future of work will be shaped by many forces; automation and AI will play a massive role. But one of the most immediate levers we have is the capacity to ask great, informed questions, to prepare for tough conversations and to put our best foot forward. LLMs amplify this capacity, but these tools still require human follow-through. So, rehearse the difficult call, draft the email, request the meeting and keep the log. Treat each ask as an experiment, not a referendum on your self-worth, and you'll soon start to see that the upsides are limitless.

If enough women do this consistently, asking stops feeling risky and begins to feel normal. Leadership pipelines widen, projects are better resourced and pay gaps narrow. The workplace starts to reflect a healthier balance, one where ambition and participation are shared, not gendered. Now that feels like proper progress!

CHAPTER THREE: HEALTH, NOT HUSH

THE UNEQUAL BODY

If you want a poignant example that shows how deeply women have been short-changed by modern medicine, you just need to look at publicly available official records. In 2020, the UK's Independent Medicines and Medical Devices Safety Review published *First Do No Harm*, a landmark report into three memorable scandals: pelvic mesh, hormone pregnancy tests and the anti-epilepsy drug sodium valproate. The review heard from hundreds of women whose lives were impacted by medical interventions sold to them as safe. They collectively described experiencing debilitating pain after mesh procedures, the decades of unanswered questions around hormonal pregnancy tests, and the children harmed after pre-birth exposure to valproate. The conclusions were really shocking, but more shocking still was the fact that these harms were actually wholly avoidable. The systems meant to protect patients had wholly failed to listen to women or act on what they had said.

Take pelvic mesh, a story that's horrified so many of us over the years. Like me, you've probably empathised and grimaced in equal measure. Women were offered it as a quick fix for incontinence and prolapse, yet many weren't fully informed of its risks. When nasty complications emerged, they fought hard to be believed. The Cumberlege Review that produced the report catalogued a pattern that felt irritatingly familiar, calling out inadequate data, weak post-treatment monitoring and a culture that was wired to question what the patients were saying, rather than the efficacy of the products themselves.

It took years for the scale of the issue to be acknowledged, either internally within the system or publicly. But the bigger lesson it highlighted wasn't about a single medication or device failure, it was about a system that didn't hear women, and possibly even actively ignored women, until the widespread harm the interventions had caused was totally undeniable.

Consider hormone pregnancy tests, most notoriously Primodos, which went on to be associated with birth defects, although the scientific picture around this one remains highly complex and contested. The House of Commons Library has been careful with its wording, noting that a definitive causal link has never been formally established, which probably means I should proceed with a degree of caution on this one, too. Yet the 2020 *First Do No Harm* review concluded that these drugs should not have remained available after 1967. Reporting by *The Times* and *The Guardian* both highlighted that women continued to be prescribed Primodos for years after safety concerns first surfaced, with regulatory action delayed and evidence downplayed. As *The Guardian* observed in 2020, "warning signs were ignored, and the women left to live with the consequences". Where the data was inconclusive, the system failed to hit pause, and the burden of proof was then carried by women and their babies.

Then there's sodium valproate, an effective anti-epileptic drug with well-known associated risks in pregnancy. The regulator has repeatedly strengthened safeguards in recent years, including new UK safety measures from January 2024 and further updated guidance in 2025. The headline figure is that around one in nine babies exposed before birth will have a birth defect, with further risks to ongoing development. These risks have been known for years, yet warnings, consent processes and prescribing practices didn't consistently inform or, more importantly, protect women. Only sustained pressure and formal regulatory action shifted things, but it took an alarming length of time to get to that point.

I also feel compelled to mention a campaign that brings the stakes of this chapter into sharp focus, called Jess's Rule. It was motivated by the tragic death of 27-year-old Jessica Brady, who made more than 20 appointments with her GP over five months relating to a range of symptoms before being diagnosed with terminal cancer. Her parents launched the petition that grew to nearly half a million signatures, and on 23 September 2025 the UK government announced that GP practices will now apply a "three-strikes and rethink" protocol: if a patient presents three times with the same or escalating symptoms and no substantiated diagnosis, the clinician must review, consider a second opinion or refer to a specialist. Prominent backers include the Royal College of General Practitioners and the (then) Health Secretary Wes Streeting. For women in particular, often the ones navigating complex health paths and advocating for themselves, Jess's Rule offers one small but powerful shift in the system: the permission to ask, and the guarantee that the system must respond. At least, that's the theory. Fingers crossed it's the reality.

It's a sharp reminder that women are often left carrying the administrative and emotional load of pushing their case forward when the system is telling them no, and yet their instincts are ultimately proven to be correct. Jess sought help again and again, so she could hardly be accused of failing to advocate for herself. But it highlights a system that appears to be calibrated to stall patients and deflect concerns, to downplay a woman's intuition. The lesson is the same as with the mesh, Primodos, and valproate scandals: when women aren't listened to, the consequences can be catastrophic.

These are *not* stories about women failing to ask, they're stories about women not being heard, and that distinction is vitally important. It would be totally wrong to claim that better self-advocacy alone could have prevented this level of harm inflicted on women by the system. The point is that when the system is slow to correct itself, the cost of silence rises. Women shouldn't have to carry that burden, yet history shows they often did and on occasions still do. And depressingly, the imbalance for women in medicine runs far deeper than a handful of scandals.

Did you know that for years women were excluded from, or extremely underrepresented in, clinical trials? In the United States, a Food and Drug Administration (FDA) guideline in 1977 effectively kept adult women out of early-phase drug studies due to their "childbearing nature". Only in 1993 did Congress require the inclusion of women and minorities in National Institutes of Health (NIH)-funded research. The legacy of that is clear – the knowledge base that still influences medicine today is skewed towards the physiology of men, with consequences that echo across diagnostics, dosing and research into pharmaceutical side effects. Europe and the UK weren't immune to similar biases in the design of studies and the recruitment of participants, either. Everything in the world of health-related research and diagnostics skewed overwhelmingly male for decades.

A lot has been written about cardiovascular care for women too, especially in the media in recent years. Heart attacks are often framed as a male problem, and the narrative is that women are more likely to present with so-called "atypical symptoms"(!). The result tends to mean delayed treatment at best and misdiagnosis at worst. Reporting from the British Heart Foundation points to a 50% higher chance of receiving the wrong initial diagnosis after a heart attack if you're a woman. That's an extraordinary figure and it can only mean that a lot of early and essential treatment is unnecessarily delayed because women present differently to men. It shapes survival and recovery and it also shapes trust in the system. If you're told for years that your chest pain is anxiety, you learn to downgrade your own instinct to query it.

Pain is another area, or pain point, where the bias is actually measurable rather than anecdotal. Recent research has shown that clinicians in emergency departments tend to make pain management decisions that disfavour female patients compared with male patients who are presenting with similar symptoms. Absolutely mind-blowing. Add to that a growing body of work indicating women experience more intense and prolonged pain, and you have a recipe for consistent undertreatment. The pattern is grossly unfair and it's also ultimately dangerous, because unrelieved pain can become chronic and life-limiting.

Endometriosis is a condition that reveals, painfully, what happens when delay becomes the default: in the UK, the average time from first GP visit to diagnosis is now reported at eight years and ten months… that's not far off a decade! According to research commissioned by Endometriosis UK and published by the All-Party Parliamentary Group on Endometriosis, this delay costs the UK economy an estimated £8.2 billion each year in treatment, lost work and reduced quality of life. Globally, a 2023 University of York study found a mean delay of 6.6 years, with some UK cases taking far longer. Statisticians might attempt to frame this as a marginal error, but these are real numbers that are attached to real women. That's tens of thousands, possibly millions, living with years of unmanaged pain and compromised fertility decisions. Women are often trying to juggle careers and other life pressures around symptoms that are repeatedly minimised by the very medical professionals we're taught to trust with our lives.

If there's something to extract from these examples, a key takeaway would be that health systems still lean towards doubt when women describe their bodies. That doubt is reinforced by evidence gaps in the science and by strange institutional caution that isn't equally applied to men. On top of all this, I'm suspicious of a potentially widespread habitual practice of doctors and consultants appearing to confuse female composure with credibility. When a woman is composed, her pain more likely gets downgraded. When she's distressed, her credibility is more likely discounted. Call it woman's instinct, but my gut tells me this potentially happens a lot.

So, what does any of this have to do with asking? Everything, once we separate institutional blame from individual autonomy. Under-asking didn't cause mesh injuries or the developmental harm from valproate. It didn't directly lead to the terrible consequences of Primodos or cause Jess Brady to die at such a young age. A hell of a lot of questions were asked in all of these cases. But under-asking *does* worsen everyday outcomes in a system that already tilts against women. Where safety nets have failed before, the questions you bring into the room really matter. That can mean asking a GP to explain a risk in plain language, and being confident enough to refuse a vague or rushed answer. It can mean requesting a second opinion early, not after months of drifting along confused as you're bounced between appointments. It can mean insisting that your pain score is logged and treated and that diagnostic thresholds reflect female presentations rather than a male default.

Every medical appointment benefits from precision and the confidence to ask specific questions, to clarify what's vague and to leave with a clear plan rather than guesswork. The medical scandals I've mentioned remind us that patience without pressure rarely moves the dial with these institutions. The research reminds us that bias is measurable and therefore changeable. The task for us now is to pair that knowledge with a habit of increased compulsion to ask and act.

Let's change lanes from history to daily life now, to where hesitation creeps in and very possibly compounds harm. These new AI tools can help you prepare for the critical conversations that shape diagnoses and treatment, for the loved ones you care for and about, but especially for yourself. Now is probably a good time to flag that I'm not suggesting you pick fights with clinicians or flex medical degrees you probably don't have. Professionals have bristled at 'Dr Google' for years, and 'Dr AI' will undoubtedly provoke the same reaction. Still, these tools exist and patients are using them. What matters is learning to ask dignified, informed questions that lead to accurate diagnosis and better outcomes – especially when it's your health that hangs in the balance.

THE EVERYDAY PERMISSION GAP IN HEALTHCARE

The big scandals make headlines because they show the consequences of systemic neglect on a mass and pretty dramatic scale. Aspects of them are nothing short of horrifying, obviously, and the media attention makes them undeniable. But for most women, the Confidence Gap in general healthcare isn't a headline; it plays out in quieter, everyday encounters that rarely make the news. It's the GP appointment where symptoms are minimised, or the stressful late-night A&E trip where pain relief is withheld. It's the specialist consultation where too much jargon closes the door on any meaningful two-way dialogue. These patterns are what shape outcomes and ultimately erode trust.

While I haven't had kids myself, I've been surrounded by women who have given birth and gone through the associated systems for close to 30 years now. I'm struck by how common stories of poor treatment, dismissive doctors and withheld pain relief are, especially in the UK. I've walked away from countless catch-ups with new mums thinking, "Christ, that sounded traumatic", wide-eyed at the treatment they received when utterly vulnerable and depending on the care and expertise of another.

When I dig a bit deeper beyond the whispered stories over a cuppa, it does seem that even the most universal female experience reveals concerning behaviours and attitudes around care. Reports from the UK Care Quality Commission describe women in labour being denied appropriate pain relief, with requests sometimes brushed off as unnecessary or inconvenient. In the US, a 2019 study in *Birth* documented how women of colour, particularly Black women, were significantly less likely to receive epidurals when requested compared to white women. These are moments where the simple act of insisting, of asking again, and if need be, recording the refusal, can alter the trajectory of care. Yet the conditioning to defer, to be "a good patient", still makes it far harder than it should be.

Fertility and reproductive health show a similar dynamic. Women navigating IVF or menopause care often describe the need to become "amateur experts" to compensate for dismissive consultations with medical professionals. Without asking pointed questions, patients can miss out on newer treatment options or fail to secure the specialist referrals that will lead to better outcomes. The quietness on a woman's part in those consulting rooms can sometimes stem from confusion, but it's also conditioning, a lifetime of receiving signals that asking too many questions makes you an irritant or a problem.

THE HIDDEN TOLL OF HESITATION

But the real kicker is that silence in healthcare carries real costs, because a delay in diagnosis is not only an individual devastation, it also quickly cascades into wider social and economic effects. The All-Party Parliamentary Group on Women's Health in the UK has reported how untreated conditions like endometriosis contribute to reduced workforce participation and billions in lost productivity. On a micro level, hesitation means prolonged pain and missed work, which has a negative effect on women's mental health and can ultimately stall careers. On a macro level, it means health systems absorb higher costs from treating advanced stages of a disease or condition that could have been tackled earlier.

I want to touch on the generational effect, which to me is not an insignificant contributor. Women often learn this tendency to hold back early in life; a mother who doesn't push for clarity about her own health in the GP surgery often models a recognisable deference to her daughters. I remember my mum's slightly apologetic energy as I was hurried in and out of the occasional GP appointment, which no doubt was instilled in her by my grandmother, and her mother before that. I've done it myself too, many times. And this is the hesitation that replicates itself, embedding across generations. Conversely, when a woman self-advocates, when she insists on a second opinion, demands further testing, or documents her concerns, she models confidence that others notice. These tiny acts of persistence eventually grow into more significant cultural weight. In short, mums, teach your daughters how to stand up for themselves!

WHY ASKING MATTERS

Wouldn't it be brilliant if women could single-handedly fix systemic inequities by simply being louder? But sadly that's definitely not the reality. The point I'm trying to make is that under-asking compounds all these nuanced existing inequities, making it easier for institutions to get away with it in a system that's been notoriously slow to correct itself. We're all acutely aware that the NHS in the UK is stretched, that doctors work under pressure with very limited time and in structures that reward speed over care. In that environment, the well-prepared, insistent question, confidently asked, can shift an outcome in ways silence simply cannot.

Some requests will still be ignored despite deep instincts to the contrary, and referrals will still be denied for seemingly illogical reasons. But the act of asking at the very least creates a record, which in turn creates opportunities for escalation. And in systems where women's health outcomes have lagged behind men's for decades, those opportunities should be considered essential acts to level the treatment playing field.

So the everyday Permission Gap in healthcare is less about spectacular failures that generate shock and headlines and more about cumulative impact – a missed diagnosis here, an untreated symptom there or a referral delayed until physical or mental damage is potentially advanced or even irreversible. The everyday Permission Gap looks like a patient nodding politely at the end of an appointment, but it masks years of potentially preventable suffering.

This is where the thought "What if I just ask?" matters most. We all want the system to evolve on its own, of course, but it rarely does, so in the meantime, asking can become a small act of personal power. Asking with laser-sharp accuracy and with confidence achieved through methodical preparation is one of the best levers available to us right now.

Now let's zoom out to examine the systemic and economic costs of women's health inequities and why the price of silence isn't borne by women alone.

THE SYSTEMIC COSTS OF SILENCE

What's the true price of a question left unasked? That's the sharper way to think about healthcare inequity. Not just the cost of misdiagnosis, but the quiet toll of hesitation: the GP appointment that ends too soon because you didn't press for deeper answers, the prescription you accept without exploring alternatives, the tests you never receive because you didn't ask what else could be ruled out and the hideous side effects that you choose to put up with. Silence costs more than time and adds unnecessary pain. It changes what happens next.

When a woman with recurring chest pain accepts the "It's probably indigestion" line without asking, "What would rule out something more serious?", the delay could literally be fatal. When a patient living with extreme fatigue accepts "Let's monitor it" without asking, "What tests can we do now?", the result may be years before an autoimmune condition is recognised. But each moment of under-asking has consequences that extend far beyond that consultation and that patient.

At scale, those silences create measurable economic and social costs; every misdiagnosed heart attack, every delayed cancer diagnosis, every missed side effect and every untreated chronic condition ripples outwards, forcing women to be absent from work and reducing their productivity. It also likely means higher treatment costs down the line, so it's a false economy for the health service long term too. But when women ask earlier and do so more directly, more insistently and more often, those spirals can shorten. Asking is a preventative intervention. It costs nothing, but its economic value is immense.

ASKING AS DATA

There's another subtle effect worth noting too, and that's the fact that in this environment every question you ask creates a data point. When women request tests and push for referrals, question the diagnosis or insist on their symptoms being logged, they generate records that eventually shape future research. Silence is invisible in the system, it leaves no trace whatsoever, but asking leaves a mark, one that accumulates into patterns that policymakers and researchers eventually use to move the system forward. In this sense, asking isn't only self-advocacy, it's a form of collective evidence-building and shared responsibility for slowly but surely improving outcomes at scale.

THE AI FACTOR: PREPARATION LOWERS THE BARRIER

This is where LLMs begin to matter. Even though they're not doctors (I stress again – far from it!), they're excellent rehearsal partners that make asking hard or complex questions easier. Confusion often kills confidence. If you don't understand the terminology being thrown at you, you simply can't know what to ask in response. But AI can strip back medical jargon, explain test results in plain English and suggest excellent follow-up questions you might not think of in the moment. It can even simulate a consultation, giving you a chance to practise describing symptoms or push back on vague advice.

For example, a woman with recurring migraines uploads her hospital discharge notes into a private LLM and asks for a summary in simple language. The model highlights that certain treatments haven't been recommended. She turns that into a question for her neurologist: "Can you explain why I haven't been considered for X therapy?"

That single question shifts her from passive recipient to active participant in her own health management.

FROM PRIVATE REHEARSAL TO PUBLIC CONSEQUENCE

Multiply this process across millions of women and the systemic effect is potentially going to be profound. If more women go into appointments rehearsed and fluent, feeling confident and ready to Just Ask, the outcomes will tilt, serious illnesses will be caught earlier and chronic conditions could be managed better. In this scenario, treatments are then offered more quickly and distributed more fairly.

The economic gains aren't theoretical. We're talking fewer lost working days, reduced emergency admissions, lower surgery rates, diminished long-term care costs – these benefits accumulate quickly. The Permission Gap becomes a structural inefficiency, not just a personal struggle. Women staying silent drains resources; asking questions costs nothing and prevents expensive downstream problems. Now that women can prepare using tools that provide clarity and proper terminology before contacting their GP or dialling 111, confidence shouldn't be treated as optional. It's both an economic and a social imperative!

THE ROLE OF LLMS

LLMs level the playing field as helpful enablers of preparation rather than as substitutes for doctors or medical specialists. They can translate complexity like baffling test results or discharge notes into plain English that allows patients to understand enough to ask informed follow-ups. They can generate targeted questions, from

"What are the side effects?" to "What alternative treatments exist?" and "Why are you recommending this one over others?" – AI can help patients create a list of relevant questions to bring to appointments.

AI also allows patients to rehearse important conversations. Using the roleplaying feature of LLMs, women can practise phrasing and anticipate pushback as if they were speaking to a doctor or a specialist. They can map possible treatment pathways too, because AI can outline typical options for a condition so that patients know what to expect and when to ask if something seems missing.

And they offer assisted neutral reflection. Sometimes, especially when your health is on the line, your emotions can cloud your clarity, so running your situation through an LLM before a conversation can identify your own blind spots and calm your nerves.

FROM EXAMPLE TO EVIDENCE

Imagine a woman experiencing chronic pelvic pain. Historically, she might have left her GP with some vague, if well-meaning, advice to take painkillers and monitor symptoms. Today, she could feed her symptom diary into an LLM, ask for potential possibilities, and generate a list of targeted questions such as: "Could this be endometriosis?", "What tests would confirm or exclude that?" and "What referral pathways exist locally?". Walking into the consultation with that paper in hand shifts the balance. It's much harder for a medical professional to dismiss specifics than generalities.

Or take the example of a patient recently prescribed a new medication. Instead of googling through contradictory forums at 2am concerned about a suspected reaction to the drug, she uploads the official prescribing information to an LLM, asks for side effects summarised in plain language and is then able to reassure herself they're to be expected. She also prepares questions for her follow-up appointment: "Is this an acceptable side effect?", "Are there alternatives if this doesn't work?". She enters the room as a partner in the conversation, rather than a passive recipient.

SCALING CONFIDENCE

Of course, women have done all this prior to the arrival of LLMs. Many have always prepared meticulously, armed themselves with printouts, diarised symptoms and walked into appointments with steely determination to get the answers they need.

The difference is scale and speed, because LLMs make preparing just so much easier. They drastically cut the time of having to manually research and prepare, and they level the field between those with the luxury of time on their hands, or those with the education or networks to help them prepare, and those without. If even a fraction of the women who currently hesitate to question healthcare professionals began entering appointments with that level of clarity, the compound effect over time would likely be extraordinary; diagnoses would accelerate and outcomes would improve. And crucially, doctors would benefit too, because clear, specific questions make consultations more efficient.

THE MECHANICS OF JUST ASK IN HEALTHCARE

Healthcare can be one of the most intimidating environments where you have to really find and maintain your voice. Medical professionals often wear the white coats and the very deep-rooted 'patient–doctor dynamic' generally means they hold all the expertise and dictate the language. Patients, meanwhile, by their very nature, are often unwell, tired or overwhelmed by their situation, meaning the power imbalance is baked in.

That's why the Just Ask approach matters so much. It turns asking from a nerve-wracking improvisation into a disciplined habit and it makes clear that confidence isn't about swagger; it's about preparation, precision and being persistent.

Here's how the mechanics of Just Ask translate into healthcare:

- **Map the terrain**. Too often, women enter appointments with only fragments of information, and that's a natural default situation when symptoms are confusing and information is scarce. Your first step should be intelligence gathering: What do you already know? What are the possible pathways for assessing and diagnosing your symptoms? What tests or referrals are commonly used for similar cases? AI tools can scan NHS guidelines, medical papers, new research or trial outlines and patient advocacy resources, and provide you with a simple map of the conditions that might explain your symptoms, the standard diagnostic steps, the range of treatments, the pathway and the likely timeline to getting back to full health.

- **Frame the value**. Doctors are trained to balance limited resources, not only their time but also the tests and referrals they authorise, which is why framing matters. A vague complaint like "I just don't feel right" is far too easy to sideline, but a specific question like "I'm concerned this might be endometriosis; can we talk through the referral process?" is harder to dismiss. AI can help here too. By turning symptom diaries into clear summaries or by drafting precise phrasing, it helps patients translate messy, lived experience into the crisp language doctors use to make decisions.

- **Rehearse**. Most people freeze under pressure. You rehearse the question in your head in the waiting room, but the moment you sit down, it evaporates. Rehearsal helps to combat the paralysis. Using an LLM, you can simulate a conversation. You describe your symptoms, let the model roleplay as a GP and practise the follow-up questions if your concern is initially brushed off.

- **Structure the ask**. The strongest asks are short, clear and lead with the key concern. Don't bury the most important issue at the end of the consultation, put it up front: "I'm here because I've had unexplained bleeding for three months. I'd like us to rule out anything serious." I've sat in so many GP appointments over the years where I've mentioned one complaint but chosen to swallow another. Why? Sometimes out of self-consciousness, often because I struggled to find the right words. And more than once simply because the energy of the consultation felt a bit off and I just wanted to get the hell out of there. AI can help you draft those conversation openers and even suggest ways of sequencing your points, so you get to the core before the clock runs out. And if you feel awkward describing embarrassing symptoms in civilian terms, it really does help when you're able to use the correct medical terminology instead of colloquialisms.

- **Iterate.** Every consultation is practice for the next. If you leave without the outcome you hoped for, write down what happened. Feed the notes into an LLM and ask: "How could I phrase this differently next time? What additional questions might strengthen my case for a referral?" Over time, you'll build a personalised playbook, your own archive of phrasing, strategies and tactics you've used in the consultation room. Iteration means a single "no" isn't the end, it becomes data for refining the next ask.

- **Scale influence.** The final step is collective. When women share their questions and preparation more widely, when they're open about their strategies with others in support groups, online forums or even in casual conversation with family and friends, the culture gradually shifts. An ask that once felt radical starts to feel normal.

FIVE HEALTH-RELATED SCENARIOS TO THINK ABOUT

Healthcare is rarely neat or predictable. It's full of waiting rooms, missed calls, jargon, and uncertainty. These five practical ideas show how LLMs can help you move from overwhelmed to organised, illustrated through short, realistic examples.

1. THE APPOINTMENT PREPPER

Scenario: A woman with recurring abdominal pain uses an LLM the night before her GP appointment. She enters her notes and asks for five key questions to maximise her 15-minute slot. The model suggests phrasing around possible causes, tests, next steps and timelines. She walks in focused, covers everything important, and leaves with a clear plan instead of a lingering sense of frustration.

How to use it: Feed your notes or symptom timeline into an LLM and ask for short, specific questions to guide your appointment. Keep them in front of you on your phone. It keeps the conversation structured and helps you leave with fewer loose ends.

2. THE JARGON BUSTER

Scenario: After a hospital visit, a patient receives discharge notes full of terms she doesn't understand: "idiopathic", "non-specific", "borderline abnormal". She uploads the letter to an LLM, which explains the terminology in plain English and suggests polite clarifying questions to ask her doctor. When she returns, she feels informed rather than intimidated.

How to use it: Copy anonymised letters, test results or reports into a private LLM and request a simple summary and next-step questions. You'll find that understanding what's written about you changes how confidently you speak up for yourself.

3. THE SECOND-OPINION REHEARSAL

Scenario: After months of inconclusive tests, a patient suspects something's been missed. She uses an LLM to simulate a consultation with a different specialist. The tool highlights alternative diagnoses and potential investigations. Armed with that, she drafts an email requesting a referral and receives one.

How to use it: Ask the model to outline how another specialist might approach your case, then use that information to frame your request for a second opinion. Don't think of it as confrontation; it's preparation.

4. THE ADVOCACY SCRIPT

Scenario: During an appointment, a woman raising a recurring concern is brushed off with "Let's give it a few more weeks." She'd already rehearsed responses using her LLM, practising calm but assertive language. "I understand you'd like to monitor it, but I'd feel reassured if we ruled out X today. Could we do that?" The tone stays polite, the point lands and the test gets booked.

How to use it: Ask the model to roleplay a cautious or dismissive clinician. Practise responses that balance firmness and respect. The goal isn't to argue; it's to be clear, prepared, and heard.

5. THE HEALTH DIARY

Scenario: A mother caring for a child with ongoing fatigue compiles months of notes into an LLM and asks it to build a concise, one-page summary for the next consultant visit. The output lists patterns, possible triggers and all prior investigations. The doctor immediately sees the picture in full and orders new tests that had never been considered.

How to use it: Keep ongoing notes on symptoms, medication and outcomes, then use AI to condense them into a readable summary. It saves time, and more importantly, demonstrates consistency and credibility – both of which carry weight in medical settings.

Each of these examples is really about levelling out the odds a little. Nobody walks into a GP surgery hoping to spar with their doctor, but being prepared changes the energy in the room. You sound more assured, you get clearer answers and you're less likely to walk out kicking yourself for what you forgot to ask.

PUSHBACK AND LIMITS

None of this is a cure-all! Health systems are complicated to navigate, they're grossly underfunded and filled with people doing their best in often impossible circumstances. Confidence and AI can help you prepare and communicate better, but they don't magic away waiting lists or the sheer strain of the overstretched NHS, if you're in the UK. The most grounded approach is to use these tools as preparation, *not* as a substitute for expertise.

LLMs can be brilliant at summarising complex language or organising thoughts before an appointment, but *they're not clinicians and never will be*. They're trained to sound confident, even when they're wrong, and that can create a dangerous illusion of certainty. Treat them as guides, not authorities. They're useful for testing questions, less so for testing medications.

There's also a responsibility in knowing when to pause and take a breath. Hospitals and surgeries operate under strict ethical and legal frameworks, and sometimes the process has to take its course. Pushing too hard can alienate the very people you need on side. The skill lies in balancing preparation with patience, clarity with cooperation. Harder than it sounds, especially when your health is on the line, but it's important to keep perspective.

One area where I want to be absolutely black and white is mental health. I do *not* endorse using an LLM for anything relating to diagnosis, crisis support or emotional safety. These systems can and do miss vital context, they cannot adequately assess risk and they have no duty of care whatsoever. We've already seen reports of chatbots giving horrendous advice around self-harm, eating disorders and trauma, and even trained clinicians sometimes struggle to catch the signs of these highly complex situations early enough. If the experts can miss it, a predictive text engine stands no chance. And if something goes wrong, there is no accountability and more importantly no emergency response. Mental health deserves human expertise and human presence. If you're struggling, speak to a professional or someone you trust, not a machine designed to autocomplete. AI has its place, but not here, not ever in my view.

What's the takeaway? Well, think of these tools as one part of a much bigger ecosystem that includes medical professionals, advocacy groups and your own instinct for when something feels off. What AI offers is structure and speed. What you still bring to the table is judgement, persistence and common sense.

WHY HEALTH MATTERS

Health is where confidence collides most directly with consequence. It's your body, your mind, your time on this great planet. The confidence to ask sharper questions or challenge vague answers doesn't just improve care; it protects it.

This chapter sits close to the heart of this book because healthcare is where hesitation can cost the most. It's where women's experiences have too often been dismissed or delayed. If more women use these tools to prepare better, to advocate clearly, to document thoroughly, we start to rebalance a system that has historically rewarded compliance just a bit too much.

Confidence in a consultation room best shows up as a quiet kind of insistence, the refusal to be rushed, the willingness to clarify, the habit of following up. When those habits scale, the system itself begins to listen differently.

CHAPTER FOUR: EQUALS, NOT ECHOES

THE NEW LANDSCAPE OF RELATIONSHIPS

Before we get into where intimate relationships are right now, let's have a look at how they've evolved. Fifty or sixty years ago, it tended to be a very typical set-up, reflective of the times. You met, you married, you tried to stay married. "Till death do us part" was widely felt to be the most important key performance indicator (KPI) for success in a relationship. Living together outside marriage was rare, often referred to, in the UK at least, as "living in sin". Divorce reflected badly on people, and while step-families existed, their stories were sometimes whispered or quietly annexed on the family tree.

Today the picture is busier and more honest, and millions of people live together without a religious or legally binding ceremony, their minds free of sins (the non-marital kind at least!). Many people now marry later in life, second marriages are common and "blended" families (a family made up of a couple, any children they have had together and any children from previous relationships) are part of the everyday now, in the majority of cultures. The idea of one template that fits everyone has quietly slipped into the past, all of which is great progress.

These changes go beyond social trends – they impact how modern relationships intersect with money, housing, work and the evolution of love and intimacy over recent decades. Take buying a home with someone. It binds together two credit histories, two careers and obligations that may last 30 years or more. If one partner steps back from work to start a family or care for a sick relative, the financial impact can ripple along for years after. Earnings might stagnate and pensions shrink, unless both people plan deliberately to prevent it. Blended families face immediate complexity: two separate households must merge into something stable enough for kids to feel secure, with responsibilities and logistics multiplying overnight.

The language around relationships has also shifted. These days we talk far more about partnership, not roles. We talk about fairness and about making choices, with the promise of equality. However, for many, it's perhaps easier said than done. Good intentions can lag as habits learned young have a way of lying dormant, then suddenly returning when life speeds up. It's easier to default to learned behaviours when pressures hit. Only today I met an ambitious, successful 37-year-old mum of two for coffee, who told me she was considering "trad wife life" because her husband feels it would be better to prioritise his career over hers. Overwhelmed with the guilt associated with realising it's near impossible for women to "have it all", she is wrestling with "what's best".

That's where this chapter begins: in the gap between what couples say they want and what their everyday arrangements quietly deliver. Clearly I'm not a relationship expert, and I have no intention of pretending to be one. My perspective is grounded in lived experience, both mine and that of the people I know best. I'm steering well clear of dating, flirting or decoding how "into you they are". There's probably a role for AI in all that, but it's a minefield I'm not stepping into here. We've already seen the risks: catfishing at industrial scale; deepfake intimacy; weird, synthetic companions designed to monetise loneliness. When technology starts shaping who we trust, love and how we connect, it deserves a book of its own.

I'm more interested in the quieter, more practical side of partnership, the steady confidence it takes to ask for clarity when things are good, to write down what you've agreed, and to protect your future selves while you still like each other enough to be generous.

SYSTEMS IN TRANSITION

When it comes to relationships in the romantic and intimate bracket, it feels like equality in language has arrived faster than equality in our social infrastructure. We've learned to speak fluently about fairness and partnership, but the systems underpinning daily life, from law and finance to healthcare and elder care, still run on assumptions built for a different era.

Law and policy still carry the weird imprint of older attitudes, and British couples living together can discover, often too late, that there is no automatic "common-law" protection around their situation. Or that pension rules were designed at a time when one breadwinner supported a household, not for an era when two people can have zigzag careers and need breaks for care. Family courts try to be fair, yet still deliver outcomes that too often leave one partner with short-term cash and the other with long-term assets that grow in the background. The tax system in many countries still treats married couples differently from everyone else. A quiet nudge towards one model over another.

Culture is in transition right now, especially when it comes to dads taking time out to actively participate and support in the early days of a new arrival. Workplaces say they value fathers who take paternity leave, and some genuinely do, while others still reward uninterrupted presence. Equality at home is in transition too. Households say chores are shared, then subconsciously and gradually default to the person who notices first. Extended families can have fixed ideas about who should give up time when care is needed for children and grandchildren. There are definite structures and norms in our traditions that haven't caught up with the way people actually live these days, and those structures shape behaviour far more powerfully than individual intentions.

THE EVERYDAY DYNAMICS OF ASKING

Hundreds of books have unpacked that relationships thrive on honest, loving communication. But relationships can suffer from the "wrong" kind of silence too. We're talking about the silence that creeps in around decisions that feel loaded with emotion or agenda: money, ambition, children, sex, loyalty to parents and the nuances of wider family politics. People learn to skirt around these topics to keep the peace, but the result is sometimes a peace that might be delicate and breakable.

Let's think about money for a minute, never not a hot topic in any relationship. Many partners split everyday costs without much trouble, the day-to-day outgoings like food, transport, subscriptions, utilities. The cracks show up further out, in the slow decisions that shape a pair of lives entwined together... like who handles long-term saving? Who tracks pensions? Whose name goes on the mortgage and why? Who owns the business you start together and what happens to it if you separate?

It's common for one person to carry the spreadsheet and for the other to trust that this is fine. According to research by the UK Women's Budget Group, only one in four couples have women managing the household finances, compared with one in ten where men take full control. The rest say they "share" responsibility, though the detail of what that means is often hazier than the label suggests. This means trust is precious, and I think it can only be enhanced with clarity. Mix in a bit of ambition and there's another quiet complexity to contend with... a job offer requiring a move to another city sounds like an individual opportunity, but it rarely is. Someone's support network will downsize, their commute will stretch and someone will take longer to find work at the same level again. Unless the couple asks, plainly, "How do we make this fair for both of us?", it's easy to drift into and through the decision-making process. And drifting along is all very easy until you suddenly notice the distance it creates and feel that it's far from ideal for your particular set-up.

The same pattern appears in expanded caring responsibilities, like when an older parent needs help, a child struggles at school or when one partner has a health issue that requires a lot of collective energy. Without deliberate asks, households revert to what looks efficient, what "makes sense". The partner who's better at smoothing chaos or spinning multiple plates rolls up their sleeves and picks up more of the physical and mental load. The partner who can stay late at the office keeps doing it, feeling they're doing their part. Neither party probably actively voted for this, but it so easily becomes the norm. By the time irritation arrives, the shape of "how we do things" has already been set.

When relationships strain a little, hesitation tends to intensify. People hold back from asking the hardest questions because they fear or dread the answer, often leading to scenarios where they compromise silently on schedules that exhaust them, so as not to rock the boat.

Death brings a different kind of silence, usually a devastating one. A partner dies and the survivor must become so many things, including a legal expert and an accountant. Often a role they might gain overnight. If the survivor handled the household admin, there's an immediate list to work through that initially dominates the grieving process. If they didn't, there's a shock that compounds grief, possibly in the shape of the realisation that some of the protection you thought you had rests on paperwork you've never seen or thought about. We forget that committing to writing a straightforward will is ultimately a kindness to the people we love around us. A set of passwords stored where both people can find them is the same kindness. A letter that explains what to do first even more so. These are small acts undertaken on a calm day that prevent intensifying the worst pain imaginable on a truly terrible one. In the UK, 53% of adults aged 25–54 have no will or have made no plans around their final exit, which highlights that we're not very good at facing up to one of the few certainties in life.

The modern family extends beyond the couple unit, of course. Co-parenting across households requires negotiation that's both steady and human, with good humour, pragmatism and flexibility. Siblings caring for an older parent must agree on roles and boundaries, or resentment will inevitably show up. Step-families succeed when expectations are clear for all involved, not when everyone's trying to guess what will be acceptable to everyone else. In all of these arrangements, asking is the way adults protect children from the fallouts created by poor decisions from the grown-ups who should know better.

PREPARATION AS POWER: WHERE AI FITS

You're probably wondering how the heck I'm going to frame a role for AI in this, but bear with me. Yes, relationships are human before they're anything else, but it's inevitable that AI solutions will increasingly show up, offering us interesting ways to improve and enhance them. Needless to say, no smart "tech solve" can repair betrayal or make two people want the same future. What a model can do, though, is make the logistics of fairness and true partnership easier.

I do think it's reasonable to think of LLMs as rehearsal rooms and research assistants in this context too. They won't replace the actual conversation, whatever that is, but they just help you arrive ready for it. You can ask for a plain-English outline of a topic neither of you has the energy to master from scratch, like researching school catchment areas or choosing your family car. You can map options before the deadline you've put off for months. And if it's a more sensitive subject, you can practise phrasing that lands without heat so you can test what you think you want, by hearing it back in a neutral voice. It might sound odd to be thinking about AI in this context, and frankly it is a bit, but if it avoids an argument or tension, then why not? My guilty pleasure is using AI to plan itineraries of trips we'll never take, and then asking Claude to distil it down into a WhatsApp message to send to my partner.

But seriously, a partner wanting to explore a pooled pension can get clued up on the pros and cons ahead of raising it. A couple wrestling with a relocation can ask for a side-by-side comparison that includes money, commute, loss of support and time for recovery, if one person needs to rebuild their professional and personal network. Parents defining a screen-time policy could ask for a draft that helps frame up the priorities around school, friendships, homework and sleep.

Naturally none of this sees you bypass making actual decisions for yourself or as a couple; it just puts the decision or the options on the table in a shape you can actually pick up and gently throw around, be that individually or together. Be aware, however, that there are guardrails and watch-outs: an LLM can mirror your bias if you only feed it your side of a gripe or issue, so you need to be specific around objectivity. It can make a poor idea sound reasonable if you push it to and it can polish language to the point that it no longer sounds like you, which a partner or loved one will quickly spot. So, use it to prepare, not to perform. Use it to make room for the other person's view, not to win an argument. Because a healthy relationship has no use for competition and point-scoring, but there are practical uses in a tool that simplifies admin so you can redirect energy towards positive outcomes and avoiding aggro.

WHEN RELATIONSHIPS END

Endings are a part of adult life. While some are calm, some are definitely not. Most require choices to be made under pressure, often at a time where feelings and reactions are intensified.

The whole situation of separation tends to combine emotion with process and admin, and divorce adds law and complexity. Weighty jargon can enter the chat and quickly dominate... disclosure, valuation, maintenance, consent order, all words and phrases that regularly get thrown around in the heat of the moment, often by people who've never really seen or used these words before. Yet they're influencing decisions that will shape the next decade of people's lives, and potentially even an entire lifetime.

Reticence is predictable and entirely understandable here – you want it to be over, you don't want another fight and you don't want to be greedy or unkind. Yet you're exhausted and still clinging to the desire to be dignified in your "uncoupling". You're juggling a million other priorities while trying to draw a line under one life chapter to allow you to embark on the next. And this is exactly when asking matters most.

I've never experienced the formalities of a marriage ending, but I'm the child of divorce and I'm in the life stage where I'm supporting friends going through complex separations. The basic questions are clear – ask for a full list of assets and debts; ask to value pensions, not only the home and the car; ask for a schedule that will work on real school days, not fantasy ones; ask to see proposals in writing; and ask for time to check with a professional before agreeing to anything.

LLMs can lower the friction at several points typical within a marriage break-up. You can ask for a translation of the solicitor's letter into plain language, you can request a checklist for disclosure so you're not blindsided, and you can model several settlement shapes and see, in simple terms, where money moves and what that means for housing and regular bills. You can also rehearse mediation so your position is clear and can be spoken even if emotion rises. The goal is to help you keep your footing while making life-altering decisions, not to hand those decisions over to a machine.

Cohabiting couples face their own complexities, because in many places there's little automatic protection if you're not married. If your shared home is in one name, the law will treat it as belonging to that person. If there's no formal agreement, the years you spent building a life together may count for less than you assumed. Despite sounding like one, I'm not a cynic; I believe that love can be generous in spirit and still make room for documents that reflect what you both know to be fair. They're not pre-nups, they're she-nups, folks.

Children change the tone and the stakes in a marriage break-up, often hiking up the tensions even more. I know from receiving-end experience that you cannot underestimate the importance of making good co-parenting plans by ensuring they're practical and kind to all involved, with zero point-scoring or tit-for-tat. They need to name school days, holidays, handover times and costs in a way everyone can follow. They anticipate exams and illness and a child who simply doesn't want to be in a car for two hours on a Friday night. They leave room for adjustment as children grow, recognising that a routine for a five-year-old might not be suitable for a fifteen-year-old. I lived this one first hand. A plan written with that level of detail prevents a hundred small arguments and you can draft the first version with a model and then shape it together until it fits.

And of course no one chooses bereavement – the most awful and often the most tragically unexpected of situations – but you can still choose how prepared you'll be. In the months after a partner dies, surviving partners often describe the simplest tasks feeling heavy and too hard. The best time to ask each other hard questions is way before you need the answers. It's such an obvious statement, but it's so much harder than it sounds. We need to ask so much in advance of the unthinkable, but very few of us do. What benefits exist if either of us dies while employed? Which pensions have survivor options? Where are the policies kept? What would the survivor need to do in the first week and who could help? A plan built with an LLM can produce a route map that you then confirm with a professional. Sadly, grief will be a reality no matter what tech comes along, but at least it will remove avoidable stress and confusion from days that are already hard. Admittedly this is not a fun way to spend a rainy Sunday, but it could prove one of the most valuable.

BEYOND THE COUPLE

Relationships aren't just restricted to intimate ones. Today's modern family is a network of people co-existing beyond a pair, and many of the most demanding asks and negotiations will be made between adults who are related but don't share a home. Siblings coordinating care for an elderly parent or adult children negotiating with a step-parent after a remarriage. Dealing with the ex-partners of loved ones with whom they still co-parent. Each of these requires an approach and tone that's steady and balanced, ideally generous and above all respectful *and* informed. A sense of humour always helps too.

An adult sibling who lives near a parent will often take on more responsibility for a parent as they age. That can be two things at the same time: loving while also unsustainable. A short family conversation every few months can lessen the burden: "Who's doing what?", "What does it cost in time or money?", "What can be shifted for the next stretch?" and "What needs to be written down?" are all great questions. Questions that can help prevent the slow build of resentment that wrecks too many adult sibling relationships down the track.

In blended families especially, the law seems to care about documents more than intentions: wills, deeds of trust, letters of wishes and nominations on pension schemes. Without them, people default to guessing what the person would have wanted, and then an atomic bomb goes off when they disagree. A fair arrangement balances loyalty to children from previous relationships with care for a new partner. That balance emerges when everyone knows the facts and the plan isn't a secret.

LLMs can make these wider conversations less chaotic and less awkward. You can assemble a simple briefing for siblings with a list of care options and costs in the local area, you can draft a calm email that invites people to a meeting and states the purpose clearly and you can create a one-page summary of a will that highlights what's straightforward and what needs a solicitor's view. You can also prepare a list of questions that will stop a gathering of family members wandering from memory to memory without landing on a decision.

THE MECHANICS OF JUST ASK IN RELATIONSHIPS

Relationships look soft on the surface, but the decision-making underneath them can be anything but. Money, time, care, routines and boundaries are practical matters wrapped in emotion, and emotion is where many people lose their footing. Even in healthy relationships, women often find themselves carrying the invisible admin or keeping the peace by absorbing the discomfort. The Just Ask approach takes the heat out of the moment and replaces improvisation with a little bit of structure.

Here's how the mechanics translate into day-to-day partnership, co-parenting, separation and the care of ageing parents.

- **Map the terrain.** Before you ask for anything significant like shared caregiving, changes to living arrangements, a financial plan or support with an elderly parent, you need a clear picture of the landscape. Who will be affected today? Who will feel the impact in six months? What are the moving parts you can't see yet? If you're unsure, ask an LLM to lay out the practical options in neutral language so you can walk into the conversation informed rather than running on instinct.

- **Frame the value.** In relationships, an ask often lands better when the other person can see how it protects the stability of the household or keeps resentment at bay. A request like "I want us to review how we divide the mental load so we're not both burnt out by Christmas" is easier to engage with than a vague feeling that something is "off". When families shift because a new baby arrives or someone changes jobs, framing the ask in terms of long-term fairness keeps the conversation grounded rather than reactive. AI can help translate a muddled feeling into a clean line that encourages cooperation rather than defence.

- **Rehearse.** Most relationship and family arguments don't explode out of nowhere; they come from poor timing, bad phrasing or two people talking over each other, rather than to each other. Rehearsal offers a dry run. You can ask an LLM to play the part of a stressed partner or an overwhelmed sibling. Let the model interrupt you or pull the discussion off course so you can practise bringing it back without escalating the moment.

- **Structure the ask.** Keep it simple. "I want us to agree how we cover care for our mum this winter. Can we look at every Wednesday and one weekend a month?" beats a rambling monologue every time. Lead with the outcome, not the story. Then explain the reasoning calmly and end with a next step. The more specific the ask, the less room there is for misinterpretation or resentment. And always write it down afterwards. Memory, like hearing, is selective; the inbox is not!

- **Iterate.** Sometimes even the clearest request won't land. People feel threatened, distracted or stretched too thin. Instead of shelving it, adjust the scale or change the timing. Maybe you start with a pilot version of the plan for a fortnight. Maybe you revisit the childcare rota once the new job has settled. Every conversation is data. Feed notes into a model and ask it where the sticking points were or how you might phrase something differently next time.

- **Scale influence.** The final step is communal. The small wins you share with friends and siblings travel further than you think. Someone uses your cohabitation checklist before moving in with a partner. Someone else uses your eldercare questions before a fraught GP meeting with a parent. A quiet nudge in a WhatsApp chat can spare someone a year of muddled resentment. Confidence circulates, and when it circulates, it strengthens.

FIVE RELATIONSHIP SCENARIOS TO THINK ABOUT

Theory is helpful, but understanding how and where to apply it is what makes change happen. Here are five practical ideas that show what confident asking can look like in the world of relationships – each one designed to be tested, adapted and reused.

1. THE MONEY MAP

Scenario: A couple with uneven incomes and different money habits use an LLM to build a one-page summary of their shared finances. It flags where money quietly leaks and highlights what they're actually saving for, not just what they *say* they are. They use the page to start a calm conversation about priorities: what matters now, and what safeguards the future for both of them.

How to use it: Feed anonymised bank data or broad spending categories into an LLM and ask for a short, neutral summary. Let the model propose two realistic adjustments that protect both partners' futures, then agree to test one for three months.

2. COHABITATION CLARITY

Scenario: Before moving in together, a couple use AI to draft a short, plain-English agreement covering rent, bills, savings, pets, furniture and what happens if they part ways. They then take it to a lawyer to formalise. The exercise itself sparks useful conversations, the sort that often happen too late.

How to use it: Ask an LLM to produce a checklist for cohabitation agreements, tailored to your country's laws.

Keep it conversational but specific. You're not predicting failure; you're protecting the friendship inside the romance.

3. THE MEDIATION REHEARSAL

Scenario: A separating couple want to avoid a combative mediation session. They ask an LLM to simulate a neutral mediator and practise summarising their positions in under a minute, followed by one acceptable compromise each could live with. The rehearsal helps them find composure and perspective before the real thing.

How to use it: State your main objective and two areas where flexibility exists. Ask the model to generate likely counterpoints and practise responding until your tone feels measured, not defensive.

4. THE SIBLING SUMMIT

Scenario: Three adult siblings are managing their mother's growing care needs from different cities. They use AI to map local care options, funding entitlements and likely costs. The summary becomes the basis for a one-hour family call where everyone commits to practical roles for the next quarter: who visits, who handles admin, who calls the GP, who researches future plans.

How to use it: Ask an LLM to outline what's available in your parent's area, from social care assessments to private options. Use that as a neutral starting point for a conversation that might otherwise get emotional fast. End by writing down the decisions and circulate them so everyone's accountable.

5. THE PROBATE COMPANION

Scenario: After the death of a parent, one sibling feels overwhelmed by the paperwork and timelines. They upload the will and relevant documents into a private LLM to generate a checklist: who to contact in what order, and what to have ready for each call. The process becomes manageable, and the emotional load is spread more evenly.

How to use it: Ask the model to break down each stage of probate into plain steps with approximate timeframes. Confirm everything with a professional, then use the checklist to delegate.

PUSHBACK AND LIMITS

LLMs can replicate bias, rationalise irrationalities, generate overly confident positions and polish your language until it no longer sounds anything remotely like you. They have no capacity to measure love or decode your family's unique brand of dysfunction. They can't appreciate where flex is politic or adjudicate who's right in a long-standing argument. If you feed them a one-sided account of a relationship dispute, they'll mirror that perspective right back at you, reinforcing rather than challenging your blind spots. Use them for structure and preparation, never for moral judgement, tempting as it might be to prove yourself right.

It's important to say, too, that there are relationship scenarios where the processes explored in this chapter don't apply at all because safety is at stake. I've assumed a baseline of mutual respect and the physical and emotional space to have difficult conversations. Where coercion, intimidation, or violence exists, even if subtle or occasional, asking more clearly or preparing better won't solve the problem. It could even make things worse. In those situations, friends, family, professionals and the law exist for reasons that have nothing to do with negotiation and everything to do with your own protection. If you're unsure whether your relationship falls into this category, that uncertainty itself is a red flag worth exploring with someone you trust outside the relationship. The only appropriate role for AI in abusive dynamics is to help you research and expedite a safe exit, quietly, carefully and with professional support if needed.

Even in healthy, supportive partnerships, better questions don't guarantee easy outcomes. If you use it to "win" it's unlikely you will win long term. You'll still have arguments which go nowhere because the necessary compromise requires both people to give ground. You'll still encounter friction points that no amount of AI-powered rehearsal smooths away. Family politics will remain messy. In-laws will still have opinions. Bereavement will still fracture even the most carefully laid plans. What preparation does is ensure that when compromise happens, it's deliberate and shared rather than quietly absorbed by the same person for years. Fairness that's visible and negotiated, not assumed and endured.

WHY RELATIONSHIPS MATTER

Relationships and the loved ones around us shape or influence almost every decision we make to some degree, about how we spend, where we live, what we save for and how we plan for the future. When couples communicate clearly and fairly, the positive effects push outward: stronger households, steadier communities, better economic participation. Confidence in this domain doesn't just build happier partnerships, it builds resilience into the social fabric.

THE BIGGER WHAT IF

At the risk of stating the obvious, women already influence a hell of a lot of life's decisions. Every home, holiday, mortgage and move is powered by the thousand quiet negotiations that mostly happen out of sight, behind closed doors. But what if those same conversations carried just a little more clarity or a touch more fairness? Even a better sense of shared accountability?

Imagine relationships where plans are written down before they become points of tension. Or where care duties are clearly defined and not assumed and where dividing the load feels like good teamwork rather than a personal failing. Those are the sorts of habits that quietly rewrite the economy from the kitchen table outwards.

Because when things run smoothly at home, everyone benefits. Fewer families fall into hardship after a split. More women retain financial stability through midlife and beyond. Children grow up watching adults problem-solve with decency and humour, which tends to stick. Men gain too; transparency has a calming effect, and knowing what's expected of you takes the sting out of resentment. Could the necessity of mind reading become a thing of the past…?!

Economists rarely talk about emotional steadiness as a growth driver, but it occurs to me that maybe they should. When households feel fair and secure, people make bolder choices. They invest, retrain, start businesses, renovate or simply plan with confidence. It's a radical thought but those decisions could flow through markets faster than any government initiative ever could.

Nobody needs more red tape in their love life, or in their wider relationships. What matters is finding a way to give them enough shape to survive the chaos that real life throws at them. A bit of clarity, a few honest conversations, the habit of asking rather than assuming... Those are the things that build resilience over time. Confidence in relationships grows quietly that way, through small, steady exchanges that make the next one easier. And when that kind of confidence takes root at home, it doesn't stay there. It filters out into how we work, lead, care and show up in the world.

CHAPTER FIVE: FINANCE AND WEALTH - THE PRICE OF HESITATION

THE MONEY GAP NOBODY TALKS ABOUT

Let's dig into wealth and kick off with a semi-positive – women control roughly 85% of consumer spending in developed economies, according to *Harvard Business Review*. They make the majority of purchasing decisions across nearly every category: groceries, healthcare, cars, holidays, financial services. Having spent over two decades in my communications and creative agency career selling goods and services across these categories, I can tell you that women, and especially mums, get a lot of airtime when people in suits (too often men!) are strategising.

Yet when you examine the data on major expenditures and the big-ticket items that move markets and ultimately shape GDP, a different pattern emerges. Women have a tendency to delay. They defer. They research endlessly but something seems to hold them back. A 2022 Lloyds Bank study found that women in the UK were significantly more likely than men to postpone major purchases like replacing a car, booking long-haul travel or commissioning home renovations, even when financially able to proceed. The cited reasons were revealing: fear of making the wrong choice, lack of confidence navigating technical specifications, anxiety about being sold something unnecessary. I'd add to that, in laywoman's terms, the likely fear of being ripped off.

In the US, Fidelity's 2023 Women and Money Study showed similar patterns. Women hold more cash in savings accounts relative to men, often parking money in low-interest products rather than investing or spending on wealth-building assets. I'm guilty of this myself. (Shout out to Laura, my financial adviser, who showed enormous patience as she "went on the journey" with me…!) My confidence in navigating financial products lags behind my financial literacy, and I suspect that's true for many women. Knowledge without confidence is like having a hiking map but being too uncertain to wander off the well-trodden path to actually use it.

The economic cost of this hesitation is real yet rarely properly calculated. If British women alone brought forward just 20% of their deferred spending on cars, property improvements and travel, categories where hesitation is most pronounced, the injection into the economy would run into tens of billions annually. That's existing organic demand, being suppressed by both the frictions of the system and the learned caution in the vast majority of us.

It would be easy to think this is about frivolous consumption. It isn't. A reliable car opens up job opportunities beyond the public transport radius, expanding the potential for a longer commute for the right opportunity. A loft conversion creates space for a home office or rental income stream. Overcoming a fear of flying might mean finally visiting a sibling who emigrated, or taking the career break you've been putting off for a decade. When women defer these decisions indefinitely, they pay a price despite holding back spending.

WHERE CONFIDENCE MEETS CONSEQUENCE

My first big expenditure was a third-hand Fiat Uno at 18. I loved that car. I juggled multiple jobs to save up to buy it, all while paralysed by the idea of making the wrong decision. I researched models obsessively, studied resale values, consulted anyone who'd listen. Then I took a dad-bracket man along with me to buy it (thanks, Gary!). That anxiety turned out to be distinctly female.

The Society of Motor Manufacturers and Traders reports that women represent around 40% of new car buyers in the UK, but research shows they take significantly longer to make final decisions – often six months or more, compared with three months for men. Women report feeling patronised or pressured in dealerships, uncertain about finance terms, anxious about being upsold unnecessary warranties and nervous about depreciation. All justified concerns, particularly given scandals like the motor finance investigation, which revealed brokers inflated their interest rates for personal gain, disproportionately affecting women who felt less equipped to challenge the terms.

The Financial Conduct Authority's intervention and subsequent redress scheme, which ran into billions, proved that hesitation was a totally rational reflex in the category. But another paradox appears in the headlights: the very systems designed to exploit uncertainty then penalise those who protect themselves by waiting. Prices rise, insurance premiums increase, models change, the optimal buying window closes. Women subsequently miss out.

In Australia, a 2023 Canstar study found that women were 30% more likely than men to delay buying a car due to "lack of confidence in negotiating price". The financial impact? Women paid on average AU$2,800 more when purchases were eventually made, because leverage had eroded and urgency had set in. Hesitation basically increased their financial outlay, forcing them to spend more.

Property tells a similar story. In Canada, the Real Estate Association reported that single women are now the second-largest group of homebuyers after couples, yet they take longer to move from viewing to offer. A 2024 survey found that 68% of female first-time buyers cited "fear of making a mistake" as a primary stressor, compared with 41% of men. Women often buy later, sometimes missing price points or being gazumped in competitive markets.

The gap I'm talking about here isn't about the ability to actually afford the property, it's about the perceived authority to act. Even women with strong incomes and clean credit histories describe feeling scrutinised differently by mortgage advisers, or talked down to by estate agents. I've fielded direct enquiries from estate agents about whether there's a husband to liaise with more times than I can count over the years. (I was most recently asked this, within the last 12 months, by a woman!) I think there's a more subtle contributor too – some women feel second-guessed by family members when it comes to money and how they spend it, in ways their male counterparts aren't. The cost for navigating all this is time, and time costs opportunity. Opportunity deferred for too long in property markets has a habit of becoming opportunity lost, especially in hot markets when competition is fierce and advantage and negotiation smarts mean everything.

Travel is where the pattern gets particularly interesting, and for me professionally it's one of my favourite categories. I often say it's in the blood, as I'm the daughter of a travel agent and granddaughter of a man who launched Jersey Airlines in the 1950s, a small airline connecting the Channel Islands to the mainland for leisure travellers for the first time. I could write a whole book on why I feel travel is vitally important in life and why I think it is one of the best things to spend your hard-earned cash on. When the toss-up is a new sofa or buying a plane or train ticket to get you somewhere new, there is only one correct answer in my book. And I'm not alone. Women travel more than men globally, according to the World Tourism Organization, yet at the same time they book quite differently. Booking.com's 2023 research showed that women spend 40% more time researching trips before committing, visiting twice as many comparison sites. That thoroughness should be an advantage, but in environments with dynamic pricing, where rates shift hourly, hesitation can mean paying more or missing availability entirely. I'm sure you have a story or two about researching flights, then returning to book, only to be greeted by an unwelcome price hike.

A 2024 study from Expedia Group found that women were also far more likely to second-guess their travel choices post-booking, particularly for high-value trips. Not because the trip was wrong and they were regretting it, but because confidence in the decision and most likely the accompanying financial outlay hadn't solidified for them. The result? Lower likelihood of rebooking with the same provider and delayed decisions on the next big trip.

What these differing categories all share are degrees of perceived associated complexity. Car purchases involve finance structures most people don't encounter elsewhere. Property purchase and rental include legal processes that feel a bit like they were purposely designed to intimidate. Travel, especially long haul or multi-country, requires navigating airline alliances, cancellation policies, visa rules, insurance fine print. Each layer adds cognitive load that, when combined with cultural messaging that women should be cautious with money, compounds the tendency to delay and therefore miss out.

This is the Hesitation Tax: the cumulative real-world cost of these delays, be that higher prices paid when urgency overtakes being strategic in your decision-making, or the opportunities missed when the timing is off because you stalled a little too long.

THE SYSTEMS THAT PROFIT FROM SILENCE

Regulators have spent years documenting how customers who stay quiet pay more. The "loyalty penalty" in categories like broadband, mobile, savings, mortgages and home insurance became so grievous that Citizens Advice brought a "super-complaint" in 2018, estimating the penalty at £4.1 billion per year. The Competition and Markets Authority investigated in detail. Ultimately, this is a transfer of wealth that stems from individual inertia and boosts corporate margins to unfathomable proportions.

Insurers were told to stop "price-walking" existing customers in 2022. The Financial Conduct Authority estimates the ban will save consumers billions over a decade, even accounting for wider price pressures. That's regulatory confirmation that asking, switching and challenging terms moves real money.

The telecoms category shows a similar dynamic, with Ofcom's Switching Tracker revealing persistently low switching rates in broadband and mobile. *Which?* reports that large numbers who try their luck and attempt to negotiate on the phone get money off. The pattern is clear: if you ask, you often save. If you do nothing, you subsidise everyone else, especially those already asking.

Subscriptions are the modern quiet drain and a special irritation of mine. Over the years I've signed up for everything from candles and pet food delivery to planet-friendly detergent. Nearly all of them took my money for far longer than I intended or wanted them to. Why? Because

I was stretched juggling everything else in my life and it fell to the bottom of the admin list. The UK's Digital Markets, Competition and Consumers Act tightens rules on auto-renewals and "subscription traps", with the government estimating the cost of unwanted subscriptions at around £1.6 billion annually. The law now forces clearer reminders and easier cancellations, but the quickest savings still come from confident negotiation.

But in reality women face a double bind. The first constraint is time. As we've talked about, women still do far more unpaid work than men, which means less mental bandwidth for comparison shopping or contract reading, or for sitting on hold for hours to semi-automated call centres. The Office for National Statistics reports that British women spend around half an hour more each day on unpaid household work than men. The Women's Budget Group estimates the overall gap at roughly 60%. So when spare time itself is scarce, defaulting to the easiest option becomes a rational and entirely understandable survival strategy.

The second constraint is that of learned experience. Many women have been told, explicitly or implicitly, that being firm in conversations about money is greedy or rude. Some older generations might go even further, holding on to perceptions that it is unattractive or unladylike. The legacy of all this today translates into us hesitating to challenge a renewal quote, to push a landlord on repair timelines or ask a broker to match an advertised rate. Ofcom's work on switching shows how the perceived hassle of the admin deters action even where savings are likely.

THE WEALTH PROBLEM

Everyday savings matter because they free up cash and build breathing space. But the larger prize for all women is personal wealth accumulation: pensions that compound, investments that quietly generate returns, property that appreciates. Wealth decides whether life feels precarious or secure, especially in midlife and beyond.

Money is what you earn and spend, wealth is what you hold and grow. The challenge is that wealth has historically been framed as more of a masculine domain. Google image search "venture capitalist" and you'll see what I mean. For too long, women have been encouraged to focus on day-to-day budgeting while being sidelined from conversations about long-term capital growth.

The irony is that women *are* good investors. A landmark study by Warwick Business School tracked more than 2,800 investors over several years and found women's portfolios outperformed men's by 1.8% annually. The reason? Women traded less frequently and resisted the instinct to follow the herd, preferring to focus on fundamentals. Fidelity's 2021 Women and Investing Study showed similar results in the US. Yet despite these strengths, women invest less often, with less money, later in life, highlighting again that the gap is far more about access and confidence over financial acumen.

Nowhere is this clearer than pensions, and the "gender pension gap" is worryingly wide. The Scottish Widows' 2023 report put it at 39% in the UK, meaning women are on track to retire with nearly two-fifths less than men. Lower salaries, career breaks, part-time thresholds and wage gaps all contribute to this. But so does hesitation: reluctance to challenge employers about contribution-matching or to ask pension providers for better options. A survey by Aegon found that only a small minority of women had increased contributions after learning about tax relief benefits, compared with a far larger share of men. The opportunity sits there, waiting to be claimed, but not enough of us do it.

Property is often the largest single asset a household will own, and here too, confidence makes a difference. Negotiating a mortgage rate, challenging service charges or pushing for clarity in property contracts can mean tens of thousands saved or lost. Yet women are statistically less likely to take the lead in mortgage negotiations even when they're co-signatories.

Inheritance presents another scenario worthy of mentioning, while we're talking all things financial. Legal charities in the UK report that widows often fail to claim full pension entitlements or property transfers, in part because they feel intimidated by financial advisers or pressured into quick agreements during grief. These decisions go on to shape wealth trajectories across future generations.

Part of the hesitation stems from how risk is framed, and behavioural finance research shows that women are more likely to describe themselves as "risk-averse" investors. Yet when adjusted for income volatility and caregiving responsibilities, the picture changes. What looks like risk aversion is often a rational preference for security in contexts where women have less buffer to fall back on. If you're paid less and carry more unpaid labour, the downside of making a poor investment looms larger.

But risk perception shifts with having quality information at your fingertips. The better informed you are, the less risky decisions feel. When pension brochures get translated into plain English, when investment products get compared side by side, when you can roleplay a conversation with a financial adviser and rehearse questions like "Why are you recommending this fund?" or "What are the fees?" or "How does this compare to the benchmark?" clarity reduces anxiety.

WHERE AI ENTERS THE PICTURE

LLMs can make the financial landscape legible in ways that compress what used to take hours into literal minutes. They can map three mortgage offers side by side, flag hidden fees, lay out the pros and cons and draft negotiation scripts. They can translate pension statements into plain English, highlighting contribution rates, projected pots, employer matches. They can run scenario models: "If I increase contributions by 2% for ten years, what happens to my retirement income?" They can reduce fourteen-page brochures into clear bullet points, because being bored by reading and trying to digest dense financial paperwork is entirely reasonable.

The key is rehearsal rather than automation. These tools give you the ability to practise the asks that feel intimidating: querying a fee structure, insisting on seeing alternatives, negotiating terms. This is wealth-building's equivalent of the preparation we explored with utilities and subscriptions, only here the stakes are measured in decades rather than months.

When a woman digs out and uploads her pension statement and asks for the three most important numbers, she finally knows what to ask her provider about. When she feeds three competing savings accounts into a model and requests a plain-language comparison, she walks into the bank clued up, assuming she's one of the few lucky enough to still have a local branch. When she uses AI to draft a calm, factual challenge to a mysterious charge on an invoice, companies tend to engage more respectfully.

WHAT CHANGES AT SCALE

The personal stories matter: a mortgage rate challenged, a pension contribution increased, an investment portfolio finally started. But it gets a lot more interesting when we think about the fact their true force is in collective accumulation. Confidence in finance, multiplied across millions of decisions, becomes a driver of growth and redistribution on a national and global scale.

Every time a woman negotiates better terms, switches providers or invests surplus cash, she sends a signal, and markets are extremely sensitive to signals. When enough consumers demand transparency on fees, financial institutions adapt their pricing. When more investors prioritise sustainability or long-term value, funds change allocations. Confidence at scale influences how institutions allocate power and resources.

Industries built on deferred demand suddenly encounter accelerated cycles, supply chains adjust, jobs follow. The British Retail Consortium estimated that women's "deferred major purchases" totalled approximately £41 billion in 2023. Even bringing forward 20% of that represents £8.2 billion in immediate-demand stimulus for the economy.

Inheritance and intergenerational wealth magnify the stakes. By 2030, trillions in assets will shift to women as widows and beneficiaries of ageing parents. If women approach these moments with confidence, asking solicitors to explain every clause, questioning fees, investing rather than parking assets in cash, the shape of intergenerational wealth changes. Children inherit not just more capital but different kinds: diversified portfolios, property with fairer ownership structures, pension pots that last. Fewer families fall into poverty after a death. Fewer older women rely on public support.

As the boomer generation exits and wealth transfers to midlife children, what recipients do with it could have seismic economic effects we're unlikely to see again in our lifetimes. If you fall into this bracket, you owe it to parents and grandparents, who no doubt worked hard for that money, to make it work just as hard for you and your children.

THE MECHANICS OF JUST ASK IN FINANCE

For many of us, financial confidence especially works less as a trait and more as a practice, a muscle that needs working to both maintain and strengthen it. If you're not a natural born numbers whizz, this stuff doesn't come easy, but at least this can seriously take the edge off.

- **Map the terrain.** Financial products seem designed to confuse and overwhelm. Mortgages span dozens of pages, pensions bury fees in footnotes, investment funds advertise performance but obscure costs. Intelligence gathering comes first. Upload three mortgage offers and a model will map differences in interest, fees, hidden clauses. Feed in a pension summary and ask it to highlight your contribution rate versus industry benchmarks. Inheritance paperwork? Extract the questions worth asking your solicitor before you sign. Mapping shrinks complexity until the landscape is clear rather than just confronting.

- **Frame the value.** Asking often gets dismissed as self-serving, particularly when women do it. The antidote is reframing. Position the ask as rational and value-driven. A bigger pension contribution tightens the belt today to loosen it tomorrow, the simplest form of long-term self-reliance. A lower mortgage rate isn't a personal windfall but an efficiency that frees resources for education, investment or spending on good times and making memories. AI can generate phrasing that shifts frames. "This rate seems above the average in your sector. Can you explain why?" is harder to dismiss than "Can I have a discount?" Framing signals seriousness, and seriousness commands both attention and respect.

- **Rehearse.** Money conversations can feel adversarial: you versus the bank, you versus the broker, you versus the adviser. Rehearsal neutralises the fear of conflict. An LLM can roleplay as a pushy mortgage adviser, a sceptical financial planner, a landlord reluctant to negotiate. Running through objections and practising responses means arriving at the real conversation less likely to be derailed. It's about getting comfortable sounding like you mean it, not learning a script.

- **Structure the ask.** Clarity wins in financial settings and vagueness is generally expensive. "I was hoping for a better deal" invites a brush-off. "Based on competitor offers, I would like this rate matched" invites engagement. AI can refine structure: condense sprawling notes into a three-point pitch, identify the strongest data to lead with, suggest an order. A structured ask takes ambiguity out of the room.

- **Iterate.** Not every ask will succeed on the first attempt. Confidence builds when you treat the process as iterative. Keep notes and identify which arguments landed. An LLM can act as a feedback loop. After a conversation, summarise what was said and ask for alternative phrasing for next time. Over months, this creates a personal playbook refined through lived experience.

- **Scale the influence.** When individual women Just Ask, they improve their own terms. When many do it, institutions shift. The FCA's ban on price-walking in insurance came about after years of consumer complaints. Car finance redress schemes emerged because people asked for investigations, which shows that regulation responds to volume. Culture only changes when asking becomes expected rather than exceptional. Banks that once relied on inertia now have to compete harder. Advisers who once dismissed questions are now wired to expect them.

FIVE FINANCE SCENARIOS TO THINK ABOUT

Finance is where hesitation costs us in a literal sense, but it's also where small efforts of smart preparation can deliver sizeable returns. These five ideas show how LLMs can turn anxiety into action.

1. THE RATE HUNTER

Scenario: Mortgage renewals are full of fine print, and loyalty rarely pays. A woman uploads two competing offers into her LLM and asks for a clean, side-by-side breakdown. The tool compares total costs, flags hidden fees and drafts a short email asking the provider to match the better deal. The tone is factual rather than pleading. Within a week, she's saved hundreds over the year.

How to use it: Drop the main numbers from each offer into a private model. Ask for a plain-language summary showing which costs repeat, where penalties hide and what the real long-term rate looks like. Then have it write a short negotiation script you can adapt for calls or emails. The clarity gives you leverage you didn't have before.

2. THE PENSION DECODER

Scenario: Pension paperwork has unique power to make your eyes glaze over. A woman feeds her statement into a model and asks for the three most important numbers: contribution rate, projected pot and employer match. The LLM summarises in plain English and flags missed contributions from a previous employer. For the first time, she knows exactly what to ask her provider about. The follow-up conversation leads to correcting an oversight that adds thousands to her retirement pot.

How to use it: Request a summary that spells out contribution levels, tax benefits and expected growth over time. Prompt it for sensible follow-up questions for your provider or financial adviser. Seeing your future in bullet points makes it easier to take action in the present.

3. THE INVESTMENT PRIMER

Scenario: A woman who's never invested uses AI to translate the brain-numbing finance jargon she's encountering as she pushes into a new, more proactive era of managing her money. Terms like "ETF" and "index fund" suddenly make more sense when explained alongside examples. The model creates a starter plan built around her risk tolerance and monthly budget. By the time she meets her financial adviser, she's fluent enough to push back on vague jargon and ask for clarity. She leaves the meeting with a portfolio she understands rather than one she's nodding along to.

How to use it: Ask the model to explain unfamiliar financial terms as if teaching a friend. Request a simple checklist covering what to research, what to avoid and which questions to bring to a professional. Confidence grows when you feel like you're in the conversation rather than just nodding through it.

4. THE BILL REBUTTAL

Scenario: A household bill arrives with a mysterious £90 "processing charge" that wasn't in the original agreement. Instead of sighing and paying, a woman uploads the invoice and original contract into her LLM and asks for a draft challenge. The model produces a three-line message that's calm, polite and impossible to dismiss. Within a week, the company apologises and removes the charge. No phone calls, no escalation, just clarity and evidence.

How to use it: Upload the document and ask the model to identify discrepancies between invoice and contract. Request a concise email outlining the issue and evidence. Tone matters here – confident and factual usually wins over furious and vague. Companies back down faster when they realise you've actually read the fine print.

5. THE FUTURE BUILDER

Scenario: A mid-career freelancer wonders if she can afford to take a year off to study. Instead of guessing or endlessly worrying, she asks an LLM to model the impact on savings, pension and cash flow. It maps three scenarios: the break, the part-time option and business as usual. Seeing the trade-offs laid out in black and white helps her make a decision based on numbers rather than nerves. She takes the year off, knowing exactly what it costs and what she's gaining.

How to use it: Feed in your income, costs and savings goals. Ask the tool to simulate what happens if you change one major variable like work hours, income, rent or investment levels. This isn't about predicting the future but seeing your options in sharper focus so you can make choices rather than drift into them.

PUSHBACK AND LIMITS

It's a reality of the finance world that banks follow rigid protocols and mortgage brokers play policy favourites to optimise their own benefit as well as yours. Pension systems remain laced with jargon and red tape that even seasoned advisers can trip over. We'll never outsmart institutions but at least we can definitely stop being intimidated by them now. These tools help you prepare with a healthy amount of common sense, but they can't replace professional advice and regulation.

Money tends to have so much emotion attached, especially when your income source sits in the "I worked bloody hard for this" bracket. Talking about money can trigger pride, fear, anxiety, embarrassment or shame, sometimes all at once. AI tools don't feel any of those emotions and it's unlikely they ever will, so it's still your job to double down on being the responsible human in the mix. An LLM will draft a perfect negotiation script, but you still have to pick up the phone. Some conversations will still land awkwardly or go nowhere at all. Progress in this space has always been incremental. Remember… it's persistence over perfection!

There's a darker edge worth calling out, too, because alongside women learning to use AI tools to prepare, financial negotiators and institutions are weaponising them to extract even more value from their customers. If AI enables predatory lenders to target vulnerable customers with personalised manipulation, if it allows insurers to price-discriminate based on behavioural data or if it helps banks identify exactly which customers won't switch and squeeze them harder, then it's simply automated exploitation at greater scale. The financial services industry has a long history of using information and data to its advantage – they are probably the best in the world at it. Giving that industry access to far more sophisticated tools while hoping consumers keep pace is naïve at best, but if nothing else, it's a motivator to keep up.

Regulation matters enormously as we move into this new era, so let's hope they get their shit together quickly. The FCA's interventions on price-walking, the DMCC Act on subscriptions and the like are all recognition that markets don't self-correct when power is this unbalanced. Individual confidence helps, but structural reform is what prevents the entire game from being totally rigged. Both things can be true: you should prepare better for financial negotiations AND the systems you're negotiating with need far stronger oversight.

There's also the question of who benefits most from AI-enabled financial confidence. If it's primarily middle-class women with time and existing financial cushions, then really we've just widened another gap. Women working multiple jobs, single parents barely keeping afloat, those without reliable internet access or basic familiarity with these tools sadly don't get the same advantages. The Confidence Gap becomes a class divide wearing different clothes. Another important reason to be honest about AI's limitations and push hard for the structural changes that actually level the playing field for everyone.

WHY FINANCE MATTERS

Money quietly governs the rhythm of most adult lives and it shapes where we live, the choices we make, the places we travel, the wider freedoms we can exercise and the restrictions we live with. The financial system wasn't designed with everyone in mind, and the knock-on effect is that confidence with money has to an extent been mistaken for privilege rather than skill.

When women learn to question a fee or ask banks to do better, they're not being difficult, they're actively participating in the system that affects them daily. And when more women participate, the system starts to shift. What was once a small personal victory becomes, in aggregate, an economic movement.

Financial confidence at scale will absolutely benefit the individual. But it also reshapes how capital moves, where it accumulates, who controls it across generations. It forces institutions built on customer confusion to compete on clarity. It converts hesitation into demand, and demand into growth that's more evenly distributed. The wealth created by asking shows up twice: in tangible savings and investments, and in the quieter cultural shift of confidence being modelled and passed on.

More radical optimism on my part again perhaps, but the hope is that the quiet financial revolution for women could just be grounded in small asks, repeated millions of times, building something that looks ordinary but isn't. Wealth doesn't just accumulate in numbers. It grows in the confidence to ask for more and in knowing that doing so doesn't make you difficult. It makes you informed, which has the potential to be priceless.

CHAPTER SIX: PUBLIC LIFE - ASKING FOR SPACE

SCENE-SETTING: WOMEN SHOWING UP IN PUBLIC

For centuries, women who dared to speak out, be that in parliaments, pulpits or local town squares and village halls, were dismissed, regularly mocked, and in many cases, punished. History records the extremes of that punishment clearly enough: women branded as witches and burned for nonconformity, campaigners imprisoned and force-fed for demanding the vote, queens and writers alike executed or exiled for daring to challenge male authority. It's called *"his-story"* for a reason.

If we're honest about it, certainly in Britain participating in public life has never been a level playing field for men and women. The disruptive and occasionally radical strategies adopted by the wonderful Suffragettes in their campaign to secure women the right to vote led to them being imprisoned and force-fed. Campaigners for women's reproductive rights have been ridiculed and branded hysterical for many decades. Even today, women who take up public roles find themselves harassed and punished in ways their male counterparts rarely are – bombarded with online abuse, threatened with violence, caricatured into silence and quite often eventually forced to give up and step down. A retired MP told me it was the "constant hum of aggression" that ultimately pushed her to quit, something few of her male peers experienced to any similar degree.

We saw this with the murder of MP Jo Cox in 2016, a moment that really exposed the dangers women in public life face, simply for doing their jobs. Years later, MPs like Diane Abbott, Jess Phillips and Stella Creasy still report daily threats that would have most of us shutting our laptops for good. More recently, Rachel Reeves was mocked for crying in Parliament, an act of empathy twisted into weakness, reminding us how narrow the margin for emotional expression remains for women in politics. These incidents form part of the background noise that keeps many women on the sidelines, cautiously weighing up the personal cost of public visibility before they ever raise a hand.

According to the Inter-Parliamentary Union, women make up just over a quarter of MPs worldwide, despite being just over half the population. In the UK, a 2022 House of Commons report found that 72% of female MPs had received threats of violence, compared with 47% of male MPs. Female journalists face a similar situation: a global UNESCO survey revealed that 73% of women reporters had experienced online harassment in the course of their work. You only have to look at the "below the line" comments of a *Daily Mail* article to see how female writers are subject to criticism that has nothing to do with their work, in a way their male peers are not.

These figures show the subtle architecture of deterrence, the quiet suppression of women participating in public life that is ultimately depriving us of more balanced agendas. They act as a reminder that permission to take a stand in public space isn't a given and remains contested ground, one generally still shaped by male expectation.

But when it comes to women questioning whether they should put their hand up or their voice out there, politics and media are only part of the picture. It extends into far wider forms of activism, from community organising and informal lobbying right through to local civic advocacy. Yet it's here that women have historically shouldered disproportionate responsibility, often very informally, as the "chief doers" that tend to get things done in neighbourhoods and communities. They run parent–teacher associations, organise fundraising for local causes and set up WhatsApp groups to tackle neighbourhood safety worries. It is women who typically launch initiatives to deliver food to the housebound elderly and women who often feel most motivated to initiate befriending services for those that are socially isolated.

Community rallying is one thing, but pointed activism is another. When the ask shifts from donating to a bake sale to pressing the council for funding or demanding government action, the Permission Gap reappears. Many women stop short, and my theory is that this is in part because they worry about being labelled difficult, naïve, out of their depth. Too political.

This frustrating dynamic shows up in local campaigns across the country. I've read about the mothers in south London who lobbied councils to improve playground safety and the parent group that pushed for cleaner air around schools. Yet in both these examples the women leading these efforts felt they were dismissed as "pushy mums". However, men weighing in on planning or budget issues? Well they're commonly called out as "community leaders". The Fawcett Society found that women campaigning locally face accusations of being emotional or self-interested, particularly when issues involve children or care. Men rarely get involved at this grassroots level, but when they do, nobody questions *their* authority in quite the same way.

There are plenty of inspiring female voices out there, so it's not that women are absent from activism. We've seen many who have stepped up, especially in recent years. One of the most visible global movements of recent times, the #MeToo campaign, was initiated and amplified by women. There were the quickly mobilised street protests that responded to gender-based violence in the UK. After the murder of Sarah Everard in 2021, thousands joined the Reclaim These Streets movement. It was a spontaneous response of grief and anger from women who were determined to expose how unsafe everyday life can still feel and how urgent the demand for systemic change remains. What feels noticeable, however, is how exceptional these cases still feel – so unusual, in fact, that they garner newspaper headlines and chatter on social media.

The pipeline that sees private irritation gradually transform into public rallying often gets clogged for women juggling multiple priorities, especially if they also lack confidence in navigating formal systems. They may hesitate, unsure how to raise funds, mobilise attention or engage the right networks. Layered on top of that is the risk of being publicly targeted. High-profile campaigners like Emma Watson, who faced threats of leaked images after her UN address on feminism, and Greta Thunberg, who has endured sustained online abuse and ridicule for her climate activism, illustrate the hostility women can face for daring to speak up. For many women at the grassroots level, the fear isn't just that no one will listen, it's also that someone will lash out.

But ironically, this is of course exactly where confidence matters most. Taking a stand and participating in public life amplifies both the reward and the risk of asking. A woman who challenges her broadband provider may save £300 a year; a woman who challenges her council on childcare funding may ultimately succeed in redirecting millions and positively impacting thousands of lives. However, the stakes feel a lot higher when speaking out publicly, and challenging the status quo inevitably invites scrutiny. When women ask in public, they shift from the private negotiation you might undertake with a landlord or utility company, to staking a very visible and public claim on power to effect change, a move that still feels off limits for many.

The arrival of LLMs introduces a new possibility here too. While they don't remove the dangers associated with the reaction to women taking a stand, they certainly lower the very real barrier to entry. They can prepare a petition in language that resonates, having scrutinised the law and drafted an easy-to-follow playbook on how to petition successfully. They can condense 60 pages of intricate policy into five bullet points or simulate counterarguments for a council meeting. They can research, formulate and help rehearse a rallying speech to ensure it will have maximum impact on its intended audience. For the woman who thinks "I really bloody care about this, but I don't know where to start", AI can be the missing bridge from silence to action. And women typically care a lot, about a lot.

What if more women crossed that bridge, moving beyond their comfort zone of localised, informal community agitation? What if the frustrations and annoyances that simmer in kitchens and playgrounds and in neighbourhood WhatsApp and Facebook groups were carried into public forums with a newfound clarity and succinctness, underpinned with a powerful newfound confidence? What if the Permission Gap shrank, not just in workplaces and hospitals, but also in the very spaces where power is distributed?

Public life has always been shaped by those who dare to show up and to ask, by people who choose to push on that closed door, be that gently or firmly. The difference now is that the tools to research, scrutinise, prepare, to sharpen your case and to amplify it are within reach of anyone with a laptop or a phone. The challenge and the opportunity is to ensure that women feel not only able, but entitled, to use them to get out there and ramp up their collective voices about irritants, big and small, that could be solved.

FROM FRUSTRATION TO FORCE

Every day, women confront and deal with the tension between what they experience as they get on with living their lives and the public systems that govern them. A commuter train that routinely runs late. A neighbourhood road where walking home after dark feels risky. A council that closes the local library despite protests. These are examples of the many daily reminders of a system that seemingly expects women to adjust rather than demand better.

Turning one of these irritations into action requires crossing a bravery threshold most men never really have to consider. Sending a letter to your MP or launching a local petition, organising a public meeting or a protest march – these are the moments where private frustration tips into becoming a public force. Women care deeply about their communities and always have, so the barrier definitely isn't lack of care. The barrier is partly the structure, partly psychological, and then there's simply the practicalities, especially time and energy.

The OECD's 2023 report confirmed what most of us already know: women globally spend on average twice as much time on unpaid care and domestic work as men, which firmly points to time being the biggest practicality factor limiting women from stepping up. In the UK, that translates to fewer physical hours to dedicate to researching a council's budget process, less mental bandwidth to draft a coherent petition, almost no capacity to schedule a meeting with an MP while also managing school runs, coordinating elderly parent care and a full-time job, let alone any much-needed personal time committed to health, wellness or pets. Women are often limited in how they can engage with and tackle big issues because their to-do list is already never-ending.

I've mentioned the unique kind of online backlash women encounter then they push themselves into the public area, and this has to be a deterrent for many. The Fawcett Society's 2023 *Sexism in Politics* report found that only 24% of women say they feel comfortable expressing political views online, compared to nearly 40% of men. It's not hard to figure out why. Women have now learned to anticipate trolling, aggression, harassment and reputational damage. Many mentally calculate that speaking up simply isn't worth the fallout.

A 2024 investigation by *The Guardian* into online abuse targeting women councillors found that 82% had received threats serious enough to report to police, yet only 11% resulted in any action. One councillor in Yorkshire described receiving rape threats after proposing a local parking scheme. Another in Cornwall was sent explicit images after voting against a planning application. The article noted that male councillors faced criticism over their decisions, but female councillors faced attacks on their bodies, their families and their right to exist in public space at all. It's far from an even playing field and women sadly know it.

A University of Bath study identified several critical bottlenecks to women participating in politics: lack of knowledge about procedure, weak networks of support and systems that default to framing politics as a male-oriented career path, which all point towards institutional barriers compounding the problem and structural design flaws that keep participation narrow.

So what's shifting now is the cost of entry. LLMs can turn a lengthy, complex council traffic document into five bullet points. They can generate a draft letter to your local MP that sounds informed rather than emotional. They can map out who needs to be on a steering committee for a campaign to succeed. The question shifts from "Can I do this?" to "What's actually stopping me?"

WHY WOMEN PULL BACK

If we dig further still, we find ourselves looking beyond the overt hostility and risk of harassment to the subtler elements that keep women on the sidelines. I think there are three barriers that are pervasive but hard to pin down easily.

The credibility trap. Women in public life face constant assessment of their right to speak. A man proposing a local traffic scheme is heard on the merits of his proposal. A woman proposing the same scheme gets asked about her qualifications, whether she's consulted experts, if she's considered all perspectives. In 2023, analysis by Loughborough University of UK media coverage during the general election found that female candidates were asked about their appearance in 34% of interviews, compared with 3% for men. Female candidates were also interrupted more frequently and given less time to answer policy questions. The message is clear: your presence requires constant justification.

The visibility paradox. Women need to be seen to effect change, yet visibility invites attack. A 2024 EU study on gendered disinformation found that women politicians are disproportionately targeted by deepfakes and smear campaigns designed to humiliate them. In the UK, an investigation by *Channel 4 News* revealed that AI-generated sexualised images of female MPs were circulating on fringe websites within hours of their maiden speeches. Male MPs faced criticism of their policies; female MPs faced fabricated pornography. The gap between professional scrutiny and personal violation is vast, and women now know it before they ever raise their hand.

The "expertise" double bind. Women are expected to be both relatable and expert, accessible yet authoritative. Too much jargon and they're accused of being out of touch. Too little and they're dismissed as lightweight. A BBC analysis of Prime Minister's Questions in 2024 found that female MPs were heckled 40% more frequently than male MPs when asking technical questions about economics or defence. When they asked about health or education, they were heckled less but still taken less seriously. The acceptable range for women's political speech remains narrower than for men, and that compression is exhausting to navigate.

A 2025 report from the Jo Cox Foundation highlighted that younger women entering politics face additional pressures, revealing that women under 35 standing for local office were subjected to appearance-based abuse at twice the rate of older women and four times the rate of men their age. Comments focused on their clothing, weight, hairstyles and perceived sexual availability and relationship status rather than their policy positions. One 28-year-old councillor in Manchester told researchers she'd been advised by senior party members to "dress older" and "tone down the makeup" to be taken seriously. Male candidates received no equivalent advice.

All this stuff hangs in the background for women considering any kind of active participation in public life; there's a seemingly never-ending stream of low-level signals that you don't quite belong, that your presence is provisional, that stepping back would make everyone more comfortable. Women absorb these signals and make rational calculations about whether engagement is worth the cost. Often, frankly, it simply isn't.

WHEN WOMEN SHAPE THE AGENDA

We've already touched on representation, and the numbers tell a fascinating part of the story. In the UK's 2024 general election, 263 women were elected to the House of Commons, 40% of total seats. In the United States, women hold roughly 28% of congressional seats. Progress is visible at least, but proportional underrepresentation persists.

What matters more is what happens once women do arrive. The mechanics inside politics either amplify their influence or suppress it. Research by the Inter-Parliamentary Union shows a consistent pattern: in countries with stronger female representation, policy priorities shift towards health, education, childcare and social welfare. These aren't "soft" issues in economic terms, they're investments directly linked to human capital and long-term prosperity.

My research highlighted what an interesting case study New Zealand is, because women have held major leadership roles there for decades. As of 2023, they made up more than half of Parliament, one of the highest proportions globally, with significant Māori female representation. Under successive governments, this balance has coincided with advances in early childhood education, domestic violence legislation and climate adaptation policy. A 2024 OECD report credited New Zealand's post-pandemic economic resilience partly to social infrastructure investments championed by female legislators during the 2010s.

Japan presents a different trajectory. In 2025, women held 42 of 125 upper house seats. The country also saw its first female prime minister, Sanae Takaichi. Her appointment cracked open one of the world's most male-dominated political cultures. Whether her tenure shifts policy priorities remains to be seen, but the symbolic threshold matters.

The *Financial Times* noted in coverage of her election that younger Japanese women reported feeling "permission" to now consider political careers in a way previous generations hadn't, demonstrating that visibility creates a very real possibility for the next wave of politically motivated women.

Rwanda's post-genocide recovery offers another data point worthy of mentioning, where women currently hold more than 60% of parliamentary seats. Recovery policies prioritised microfinance for women and school access for girls. Two decades on, literacy and life expectancy have both climbed dramatically. The World Bank described it as "inclusive growth in practice", showing that social capital compounds as effectively as financial capital when women have authority to allocate it.

Contrast that with policy shifts in the United States, where reproductive health rollbacks have measurable economic consequences. A 2023 Brookings Institution study estimated that restrictions on reproductive rights will cost the US economy $105 billion annually in lost wages and productivity, along with the associated healthcare costs. So we can confidently conclude that when women's autonomy contracts, so does economic dynamism, and the correlation really is glaringly obvious.

In the UK, a 2024 investigation by *The Times* into government spending priorities found that services disproportionately used by women, spanning not only childcare, but also domestic violence support and sexual health clinics, had seen budget cuts of 35% since 2010, while defence spending increased 18% in the same period. Female MPs across parties had repeatedly flagged the disparity in parliamentary debates, often to sparse attendance and minimal media coverage. One Labour MP told the paper, "We're shouting into a void. The men in the room simply don't see these as priority issues because they don't personally rely on these services."

The pattern is visible at the local government level too. Research from the Local Government Association in 2024 found that councils with gender-balanced leadership were 30% more likely to maintain libraries, children's centres and community health services during budget cuts, while male-dominated councils prioritised infrastructure projects like road improvements and commercial development. All this demonstrates to me that women in leadership rooms ask different questions because they navigate different realities and are arguably closer to the coalface than men.

WHERE TECHNOLOGY LOWERS BARRIERS

One of the big positives now is that political preparation today looks entirely different to how it did a decade ago. For a woman considering putting herself forward publicly, be that lobbying for a cause or standing for office, an LLM can quickly map campaign timelines and flag media-risk scenarios; it can simulate a hostile debate and assist with drafting a first manifesto. Running for office demands a lot of research-heavy policy work, candidate preparation, media training, compliance checks and supporter outreach. Much of this once required specialist help and serious funding. Accessible AI tools lower both the practical and financial barriers to entry. They cut hours once spent rewriting position papers, reduce reliance on consultants, strip back the need for expensive strategy support and supercharge research.

For women who already carry disproportionate domestic and financial responsibilities, I think that shift really matters. When the cognitive or financial cost of preparation is reduced, participation rises. What once felt out of reach becomes both logistically and economically possible, which has to be an important motivator.

Real-world cases hint at what might become a lot more normal. In Kenya's Machakos County, an AI-powered civic-tech platform called Sauti ya Bajeti allows women, youth and working professionals to access budget and policy documents via WhatsApp and engage in inclusive deliberation. In the UK, several grassroots campaigns have used AI to analyse decades of local council meeting minutes, exposing patterns of underfunding for women's services that had previously been invisible and therefore impossible to calculate. A group in Leeds used this data to force a council debate on childcare provision that resulted in £4 million being reallocated. In the US, organisations like the Matriots PAC are mobilising women candidates and building support networks especially for them. These examples may represent the early frontier of a broader shift: preparation becoming scalable, entry costs falling, more women asking and acting as a welcome result.

The psychological barrier matters as much as the practical one. Many women avoid public life not because they lack ideas but because for one reason or another they doubt their right to voice them. Tools that compress the research time and generate professional-standard outputs create confidence. You're not improvising in the council chamber, you're presenting material you've tested, refined and rehearsed. That distinction is what converts hesitation into action.

THE MECHANICS OF JUST ASK IN PUBLIC LIFE

Public life demands precision because the stakes are high and the audience, especially the media, tends to be unforgiving. The Just Ask framework applies here with particular force.

- **Map the terrain.** Before launching a campaign or standing for office, understand the landscape. Who holds power? What are their priorities? Where have similar efforts succeeded or failed? LLMs can scan council meeting minutes, analyse voting records, identify which arguments have historically swayed decision-makers. A woman campaigning for better street lighting doesn't need to reinvent the wheel. She can ask an AI tool to pull examples of successful safety campaigns from other boroughs, note the language used, identify the budget lines targeted. Intelligence gathering turns vague frustration into strategic clarity.

- **Frame the value.** Public institutions respond to arguments framed in their own language. A petition demanding "better childcare" is easier to ignore than one stating "early-years investment returns £7 for every £1 spent, reducing long-term welfare costs and increasing workforce participation". AI can translate emotional urgency into evidential weight. It can draft submissions to public consultations that cite precedent, reference legislation, and quantify impact. The ask stops feeling like a complaint and starts sounding like policy.

- **Rehearse.** Public speaking, whether at a council meeting or a campaign rally, only ever improves with practice. LLMs can simulate hostile questioning, generate counterarguments, test phrasing for clarity and impact. A woman preparing to challenge her council over school funding cuts can rehearse responses to "Where will the money come from?" or "Haven't you considered X?" When the real meeting arrives, she's already heard the objections and practised staying calm under pressure. Confidence comes from preparation, not personality.

- **Structure the ask.** Public asks need to be crisp, specific and actionable. Lead with the outcome you want, support it with evidence, propose a clear next step. Avoid emotional appeals that are vulnerable to dismissal as "hysterical" or "unreasonable". AI can help structure submissions, petitions and speeches so they land with authority. A well-structured ask is harder to ignore and easier to act on.

- **Iterate.** Public campaigns rarely succeed on the first attempt. Track what works, what generates media attention, which arguments sway undecided voices. Feed that data back into your preparation and refine the approach. AI can analyse response patterns, suggest adjustments, identify emerging opportunities. Iteration turns a single failed attempt into a sustained, strategic campaign.

- **Scale influence.** Share tactics with other women. When multiple people adopt these methods, the culture of public engagement shifts. Councils accustomed to vague complaints start encountering evidence-rich challenges. Media outlets that once ignored local campaigns find themselves facing coordinated, articulate pressure. Politicians who dismissed women's concerns as "special interests" discover those concerns now come backed by data and public support. At scale, asking stops being disruptive and becomes expected.

FIVE PUBLIC LIFE SCENARIOS TO THINK ABOUT

The thought of showing up and taking part in public causes and conversations feels quite alien until you see how accessible it actually is. These five examples show how preparation turns intimidation into action.

1. THE COUNCIL CHALLENGER

Scenario: A mother notices that her local council has quietly cut funding for youth services while increasing spending on commercial development. She's angry but doesn't know where to start. She uses an LLM to analyse five years of council budget documents, identifying exactly where youth funding has dropped and what's replaced it. The model generates a three-page briefing with graphs, precedents from neighbouring councils that maintained youth services, and draft questions for the next public council meeting. She attends, asks her questions calmly and specifically, and the local paper covers it. Within two months, the council reverses part of the cut.

How to use it: Feed council budget PDFs into an LLM and ask it to track spending changes over time in specific categories. Request a summary that highlights disparities, suggests questions and identifies which councillors to target. Being prepared helps convert your frustration into leverage you can use.

2. THE PETITION DRAFTER

Scenario: A neighbourhood group wants to petition for better street lighting after several women report feeling unsafe walking home. They've tried before but the petition was dismissed as too vague. This time, they use AI to research crime statistics for the area, lighting standards from the local authority's own guidelines, and case studies from areas where improved lighting reduced incidents. The model drafts a petition that's precise, evidence-based and hard to ignore. It gathers 2,000 signatures in three weeks and the council agrees to a review.

How to use it: Ask the model to structure a petition that opens with the specific ask, supports it with local data and precedent, and ends with a clear action the authority can take. Evidence-rich petitions get taken seriously. Vague appeals for action don't.

3. THE MEDIA AMPLIFIER

Scenario: A campaign to save a local library isn't getting media attention despite strong community support. The organiser uses an LLM to draft a press release that has a compelling, newsworthy angle, by framing a link between council cuts and dropping literacy rates. It pulls in education data and quotes from literacy charities. She emails it to local journalists with subject lines that the model suggested will maximise impact with the recipient. Two outlets run the story. Suddenly the council is on the defensive and the library gets a reprieve.

How to use it: Feed background information into the model and ask it to draft a press release that journalists will actually read and consider both relevant and newsworthy. Request three headline options and five different angles depending on the outlet. Media coverage shifts power dynamics faster than almost anything else.

4. THE DEBATE REHEARSAL

Scenario: A woman is standing for her local council but dreads the town hall event where candidates face public questions. She's knowledgeable but knows that she freezes under pressure. She uses an LLM to roleplay a hostile questioner, running through 20 rounds of challenging questions on local issues: budget cuts, planning decisions, transport. By the time the real public Q&A arrives, she's heard every variation. She stays calm, answers clearly and wins her seat.

How to use it: Train the model on local issues and ask it to simulate aggressive questioning. Practise until your answers are automatic. Confidence under pressure comes from repetition, not personality.

5. THE POLICY BRIEF

Scenario: A women's advocacy group wants to influence their MP's position on childcare funding ahead of a parliamentary vote. They use AI to create a two-page policy brief citing economic research, local impact data and quotes from constituents. The brief is professional, specific and actionable. The MP references it in debate and votes accordingly. The group realises they can do this on multiple issues without needing expensive consultants.

How to use it: Ask the model to condense complex policy arguments into a format busy MPs will actually read. Lead with the ask, support with evidence, make it easy to act on. Politicians respond to constituents who sound informed because it's politically risky to ignore them.

PUSHBACK AND LIMITS

None of this removes the real dangers women face in public life. AI can help you prepare a campaign, but it won't stop the online or real-world abuse you encounter after you speak at a council meeting. It can draft a compelling petition, but it won't prevent newspapers from focusing on what you wore rather than what you said. It can simulate hostile questioning, but it won't make the actual hostility any less exhausting.

The grim reality is that the harassment women face in public life is sadly escalating, not diminishing. A 2025 report from Amnesty International found that online abuse targeting women in politics had increased 65% since 2020, with AI-generated deepfakes becoming a primary weapon. The tools that enable women's preparation are the same tools being used to fabricate sexually explicit images, generate fake quotes and spread coordinated disinformation campaigns. The playing field isn't level and sometimes it's actively hostile.

There's also the risk that AI-enabled participation becomes another form of unpaid labour expected of women. If the barrier to entry drops, does that mean women are now supposed to do even more community organising, campaign management and civic advocacy on top of everything else? The danger is that accessible tools become an excuse for institutions to demand more from volunteers rather than funding proper support. Women shouldn't need to become AI-fluent policy experts just to get their council to fix a pothole.

Class and access matter too. Women with digital literacy, reliable internet, time to learn these tools will benefit disproportionately. Working-class women, women juggling multiple jobs, those without technological confidence or resources – they don't get the same advantages. The gap between who can participate and who can participate effectively might narrow in some places while widening in others. That's not empowerment, that's just replicating existing hierarchies through new means.

The psychological toll of sustained public engagement is real and rarely acknowledged. Campaigning is exhausting. Standing for office is brutal. Even local activism, the kind that feels manageable, can consume your life. Women who step into public roles often burn out not because they lack commitment but because the cost of visibility is too high. AI can help with preparation, but it can't protect you from the rage that lands in your inbox, the coordinated pile-ons, the casual misogyny dressed up as political debate. Some women will decide, entirely rationally, that it's not worth it. That's not individual failure, that's system design.

WHY PUBLIC LIFE MATTERS

Public life is where priorities get set and where the money we pay in taxes gets deployed. It's where community resources get allocated, and ultimately where futures get shaped. When half the population is subtly yet systematically discouraged from participating, the resulting decisions reflect a partial reality. It might be provocative to say it, but budgets that ignore childcare, transport systems designed around male commuting patterns, planning decisions that prioritise commercial development over community safety are depressing but predictable outcomes that tie directly to who's in the room when these decisions get made.

Women's underrepresentation in public life costs everyone. Yes it's unfair, but perhaps the more compelling point is that there are measurable economic and social inefficiencies. The IMF found that a 10% increase in female parliamentary representation correlates with a 2% increase in GDP per capita over time, linked to better oversight of spending, stronger anti-corruption measures and longer-term planning horizons. When women have power to allocate resources, investments shift towards infrastructure that's people-oriented: healthcare, education, housing, safety. Things that are the fundamentals of well-functioning economies.

Not many of us are born activists, and the confidence to participate in public life doesn't emerge spontaneously; it gets built through small acts repeated until they feel normal. A woman who successfully challenges her council over one issue becomes more likely to challenge over another. A woman who sees a peer launch a petition thinks, "I could do that too." Confidence spreads through networks, particularly when the tools that lower barriers are shared rather than hoarded.

Public life is where the Permission Gap shows up most visibly and where closing it has the widest impact for society. When women ask for space in public decision-making, they change what institutions consider normal, what questions get asked and whose experiences count as evidence. The shift happens gradually, through accumulated asks that eventually become too persistent to ignore.

Women have always cared about their communities. What's changing is the cost of converting that care into action. The question isn't whether women are capable of participating in public life, the question is what happens when millions more decide it's finally worth the risk.

CHAPTER SEVEN: THE CARE ECONOMY – CONFIDENCE IN AGEING AND SUPPORT

THE CALL NOBODY'S READY FOR

The phone rings early on a weekday morning. A parent's neighbour, apologetic but firm: "I think you need to come. They're not coping."

Although you've been trying to ignore it, you've noticed things slightly slipping for months. It could be meals skipped or bills paid twice or not at all, it could be the same story told three times in one conversation. But "not coping" is the phrase everyone dreads, because it makes the situation suddenly, undeniably real. Within days you're trying to fast-track your fluency in acronyms you've never heard before: CHC, FNC, DOLS, NHS Continuing Healthcare. Means-tested thresholds. Domiciliary care packages. Power of attorney, which you should have sorted years ago but nobody ever brought up.

Us Brits are particularly bad at this part, don't you think? Most families know ageing parents will eventually need help, yet fewer than one in five have discussed care preferences before something forces the conversation, according to Age UK. I guess we avoid it because it feels morbid and because nobody wants to imagine their capable parents becoming dependent. For many, even broaching the subject feels like an accusation of decline. So we ignore the inevitable and get far too comfortable doing so, which means we wait until a fall, a stroke, a moment of confusion or a life-altering diagnosis occurs. Then suddenly we're making enormous decisions under pressure with no preparation and very little time.

This then likely triggers your introduction to "the system" – and you discover that the thing that's supposed to support you and offer help can feel designed to wear you down and exhaust you into giving up. Council websites bury critical information in 20-page PDFs written in policy language. Phone numbers ring out or redirect to other departments. Eligibility criteria seem to shift depending on who you speak to. Even professional communicators with time and gritty determination find themselves navigating this stuff in the dark, tearing their hair out, wondering why it's so hard.

Confidence in this context has nothing to do with personality traits. Access to information that should be public but feels withheld is what ultimately determines whether you can advocate effectively. Knowing which questions unlock which doors can mean the difference between thousands of pounds saved or lost, between adequate care and a parent trapped in crisis, and between maintaining or losing your sanity.

Millions of people, especially women, are living some version of this right now. The World Health Organization projects that by 2050, the number of people aged 60 and older will double to 2.1 billion, outnumbering children under 14. In the UK, one in four adults will be over 65 by the mid-2030s. The Office for National Statistics reports that nearly 5.7 million people now provide unpaid care, many of them women in midlife who are balancing jobs, children and ageing parents. The Health Foundation valued this informal care at over £170 billion annually in 2024, more than most government departments' entire budgets.

The UK sits in the middle of a global care crisis. Japan, where 28% of the population is already over 65, has declared itself a "super-aged society" and pays family members to provide care because the formal system can't cope. Germany's mandatory long-term care insurance, introduced in 1995, still can't keep pace with demand. The United States offers no federal paid family leave and has means testing so punitive that medical bankruptcy from care costs is common. Australia's Aged Care Royal Commission in 2021 exposed systemic neglect across the sector, yet meaningful reform remains agonisingly slow. France's allocation system is more generous than Britain's, but still relies on families to bridge the gap. Right now every wealthy nation is discovering the same painful truth: we've built societies that help people live longer without building the infrastructure to help them live well in those extended years. And it doesn't look like it'll improve anytime soon.

But behind those numbers sits a vast, often unacknowledged labour force: daughters project-managing medications and appointments, partners navigating benefit forms, adult children having impossible conversations about driving licences and house keys. The care economy is undoubtedly propped up by private effort underwritten by love, and the consequences are economic as much as personal.

This chapter focuses primarily on caring for elderly parents because that's the demographic reality defining this century, and because I know the realities of it firsthand. The sandwich generation gets substantial attention too, because that's where the load becomes unbearable for so many and it's increasingly in the spotlight. I tread lightly around parenting, especially parenting children with complex needs, because it's a world I'm not familiar with and an area where it would probably be unhelpful to make assumptions. But what connects all three is the administrative chaos that compounds emotional strain, and how tools now exist to potentially make that chaos slightly more manageable.

I see it like this – confidence in care situations comes down to having enough clarity to ask the right questions before you're too exhausted to ask anything at all. Technology won't fix the care crisis, but it can dismantle one of its least visible barriers: the information complexities that keep people overwhelmed and systems unaccountable.

CARING FOR ELDERLY PARENTS: INSIDE THE MAZE

The individual scenario attached to an elderly parent rarely announces itself clearly. For a lot of adult kids there's no single moment when someone stops being independent, just a series of small incidents: a fall, a missed medical appointment, confusion over dates, the fridge full of food past its sell-by date. By the time you realise intervention is needed, you're already sensing you're in some way behind.

Then comes the discovery that there isn't actually "a system", more a patchwork of systems that don't communicate with each other. In the UK, the NHS handles acute medical needs but not ongoing care. Local councils assess for social care, but every council has different criteria and waiting times. Private providers fill gaps but at costs most families haven't budgeted for. Voluntary organisations offer support, but finding them requires knowing they exist. The boundaries between all of this tend to feel deliberately blurred, often because at an institutional level, nobody wants to admit which budget should be paying.

I'm pretty sure every country has built its own version of this maze, just with different acronyms. Americans face the Medicare–Medicaid split, which is somehow even more byzantine than the NHS–council divide. Australians struggle with the My Aged Care portal, so notoriously difficult to navigate that private services have emerged specifically to help people use it. Canadians must decode entirely different systems in different provinces. The pattern repeats: care split between health and social budgets, eligibility determined by postcode or zip code, families discovering the mountain of complexities far too late.

In 2025, according to LaingBuisson's latest report, the average cost of nursing home care for older people in England (self-funded) is about £1,372/week (£71,000/year). In London and the South-East the level is higher (£1,513/week, or £78,700/year). Residential care without nursing support averages around £1,042/week, so that's £54,000/year.

These figures place the UK roughly mid-pack globally. In the United States, nursing home care averages $100,000–150,000 annually, driving tens of thousands of families into unexpected bankruptcy each year. Australia's costs sit at AUD $60,000–80,000, with similar asset tests that penalise people just above thresholds. Canada's system varies wildly. Some provinces cover hospital care but not "custodial" support, creating a patchwork as confusing as and not dissimilar to England's postcode lottery. The pattern repeats across developed nations: care costs have risen faster than wages, faster than pensions, faster than families can plan for.

Most people discover these figures far too late – often after a hospital discharge when someone in a meeting or consultation says, "She's medically fit but can't go home alone," and suddenly you're expected to have a plan. The assumption is that "something will work out", and by the time it becomes clear nothing will work out without significant money and a lot of stress and effort, choices have already narrowed.

Means testing creates its own rabbit warren of complexities to burrow through. In England anyone with capital over £23,250 must pay the full cost of their residential care; those with capital between £14,250 and £23,250 receive partial support (the state contributes once assumed "tariff" income and actual income have been assessed). A person's home is included in the asset test if they move into permanent residential care (unless a spouse or dependent relative remains living there). The thresholds haven't moved meaningfully in over a decade, while care costs have skyrocketed. Families just over the line can burn through savings in months, while those just under get support. A 2023 investigation by *The Times* found that thousands of families were selling homes unnecessarily because they didn't understand which assets get disregarded and were unaware that the NHS has a separate funding stream for people with significant health needs.

It's worth mentioning that NHS Continuing Healthcare is one of the system's best-kept secrets. CHC funding covers the full cost of care for people whose primary need is healthcare rather than social care. Eligibility is assessed using something called the Decision Support Tool, a points-based system that evaluates needs across 12 domains. It's complex, subjective, and according to Carers UK research, fewer than one in ten eligible families ever successfully claim it. The majority of families scoping out their options don't even know it exists. Those who do often get rejected at first assessment, not because their relative doesn't qualify but because the form wasn't filled out correctly or the evidence wasn't framed in the right way.

A BBC investigation in 2024 highlighted the postcode lottery that makes everything harder, revealing how care provision and eligibility vary wildly between councils, sometimes between neighbouring boroughs. One authority might provide 12 hours of domestic care per week; another might offer four for the same level of need. Waiting times for assessments range from two weeks to six months. Living in the wrong area means paying more and waiting longer for less support. Nobody explains any of this up front. You discover it when you're already drowning in logistics and trying to piece together nonsensical rules.

Geography compounds the problem even more, because these days adult children often live anywhere from a significant drive to several hours away from ageing parents, close enough to feel responsible but too far to adequately manage daily issues. Siblings who do live nearby bear a disproportionate load, fielding emergency calls, attending appointments, picking up shopping and prescriptions, checking in every day. A 2023 study published in the *Journal of Family Issues* found that proximity was the single strongest predictor of who became the primary carer, though gender determined how much of the actual hands-on work got done versus how much got delegated. Brothers coordinated. Sisters showed up.

Power of attorney is something that gets left far too long, sometimes until someone no longer has the mental capacity to even grant it. The legal document gives someone authority to make financial and health decisions on another person's behalf, but dementia, stroke or sudden cognitive decline can make a person legally unable to sign. At that point, families have to apply for deputyship through the Court of Protection, a process that can cost thousands and requires ongoing court oversight, which can take months. Hospital discharge often happens before families have sorted any of this. Someone goes in after a fall, gets declared "medically fit" three days later, and you're told to collect them by noon. But home isn't safe any more. Stairs are a problem, the bathroom's upstairs, there's no grab rail. The discharge team mentions "intermediate care" or "reablement services" but doesn't explain how to access them, or that funding only lasts six weeks, or what happens after that. A 2023 Care Quality Commission report found that 40% of emergency readmissions within 30 days were linked to inadequate discharge planning, often because families didn't understand what support was available or how to activate it.

Worryingly, financial abuse sits quietly in the background of many eldercare situations. Older people are now targeted by scams at extraordinary rates, and the Financial Conduct Authority estimated in 2024 that financial abuse of older adults costs the UK around £1.4 billion annually, much of it unreported.

Then there's the stress and slow grief of watching someone you love fade. Dementia doesn't take a person all at once but in increments: memory first, then recognition, then language, then the shape of who they were as a person. Alzheimer's Research UK reports that one in three people born in the UK today will develop dementia in their lifetime. Currently there's no cure, no meaningful treatment, just a long erosion that falls hardest on whoever's providing care. You're mourning someone who's still alive, and the system offers almost nothing to help with that.

Confidence can collapse in this context, not from overwhelming emotions, but from information overload and bureaucratic exhaustion. Professionally capable people find themselves paralysed. The jargon is relentless: domiciliary care, reablement, safeguarding, intermediate care, Deprivation of Liberty Safeguards. Every term has a specific meaning that determines access to funding or services, but nobody hands you a helpful glossary. You learn by making mistakes, missing deadlines, filling out forms incorrectly and starting over, bouncing around departments on the phone.

WHERE TECHNOLOGY CAN LOWER THE BARRIER

LLMs become extremely useful here, primarily as translators and navigators. One of the biggest tensions in elder care is almost entirely administrative. Compassion doesn't run out first, patience does, worn down by forms and contradictory information from different parts of the system. But AI can help in an unexpected way.

A daughter navigating her father's dementia diagnosis could upload anonymised NHS discharge paperwork into a private LLM and ask for a plain-English summary of what the consultant actually said, with suggested questions to ask at the next appointment. She could feed local authority guidance into ChatGPT and request a bullet-point breakdown of what support is means-tested and what isn't. She could simulate a financial assessment conversation, rehearsing how to ask about disregarded assets or top-up fees without the embarrassment that stops people asking in real meetings.

Whether you're decoding CHC eligibility in Leeds or Medicare coverage in Ohio or aged care packages in Melbourne, the fundamental task is the same: making opaque systems legible before you're too exhausted to fight them. AI tools can now navigate these systems regardless of jurisdiction, translating bureaucratic complexity into something us humans can actually use. Someone preparing for an NHS Continuing Healthcare assessment could ask the model to explain the Decision Support Tool domains in straightforward language, then draft responses that align with clinical criteria without exaggerating or underselling needs. Families challenging a rejected CHC claim could use AI to analyse the decision letter, identify weak points in the reasoning and draft an appeal that cites relevant case law and policy guidance.

The financial maze becomes slightly more navigable when you lean on these tools for help. A family preparing for power of attorney could ask the model to outline the difference between "joint" and "several" decision-making powers, what happens if attorneys disagree and which decisions need specific authority. Someone trying to understand care home contracts could upload the terms and ask which clauses are negotiable, what "top-up fees" actually mean, what happens if the money runs out. These questions determine whether someone spends their final years in adequate care or in crisis.

Practical logistics also benefit. An LLM can generate a medication schedule that's easier to follow than a pile of prescription labels. It can draft a clear, calm email to siblings explaining what help is needed and when, cutting through the emotion that makes family conversations difficult. It can create a checklist of what to bring to a care assessment so nothing important gets forgotten. It can even help prepare for the conversation about giving up the car keys or moving into supported housing, phrasing suggestions in ways that preserve dignity and keep the topic as neutral as possible.

A 2024 OECD report on long-term care found that administrative complexity was one of the top three deterrents to families seeking formal support. Every unnecessary form, every unclear policy acts as a barrier to early intervention. Early intervention is cheaper for the state and better for the person. Simplifying access makes economic sense even before it makes moral sense.

We've already talked about the fact that women make up nearly 60% of unpaid carers globally. In the UK, women are twice as likely as men to reduce working hours or leave employment entirely when a parent needs care. That has cascading effects on lifetime earnings, pensions and mental health. The confidence to ask for flexible work, to navigate care assessments, to challenge incorrect bills from care agencies becomes a survival skill. LLMs strengthen that capacity by making the preparatory work less daunting: drafting letters, summarising options, generating scripts for difficult conversations with employers or providers.

A 2022 London School of Economics analysis found that every £1 invested in carer support services yields up to £4 in economic returns through higher productivity and reduced healthcare demand. If even a fraction of the millions of unpaid carers had faster routes to reliable information, their stress would drop, their workforce retention would rise, their relatives would receive better and earlier care. The cumulative effect would reshape both family economics and public spending.

THE SANDWICH GENERATION: CARING IN TWO DIRECTIONS

The generation caring simultaneously for ageing parents and dependent children has become the backbone of modern family life. The Office for National Statistics reported in 2024 that one in four people in their forties and fifties now provide regular care in both directions, upwards and downwards. Women represent nearly two-thirds of that number. Many work part-time or have left work entirely as responsibilities close in on them. Employers talk about flexibility, but few have adapted meaningfully to what this dual load actually costs in time, energy and income.

The sandwich generation crisis isn't uniquely British. In Japan, "kaigo rissoku" (care leave) exists on paper but social stigma means women rarely use it, instead exiting work permanently. South Korea's combination of eldercare pressure and childcare costs has been called out as a meaningful contributing factor to the sizeable birth rate decline, with South Korea's birth rate currently the lowest in the world. Italy and Spain's "familism" culture means daughters are expected to provide care, and employment rates for women aged 40–55 are falling as a result. Even the United States, with its Family Medical Leave Act, offers only unpaid leave that most carers can't afford to take. Geography changes the details – which family members, which cultural expectations, which inadequate policies – but the pattern of women absorbing the care crisis while economies count them as "economically inactive" repeats across continents.

OECD data shows that women perform around two hours more unpaid care work per day than men across developed economies, a gap that widens sharply during the peak caring years of midlife. In the UK, the Carers Trust reports that around 1.3 million adults are caring for children and older relatives at the same time. For women who had children later and now find themselves parenting teenagers while also managing a parent's decline, this has become the norm rather than the exception.

A woman in her forties might duck out of work meetings to call her father's GP surgery for test results, then switch to negotiating with her daughter's school over exam room support. She logs off early to meet an occupational therapist at her mother's house, then spends the evening filling out online forms for both Child Benefit reassessments and Attendance Allowance applications. Each system has its own portal, its own paperwork, its own waiting times. None of them talk to each other – that would be far too convenient. The pain point is administrative but the exhaustion is still very much human.

A 2024 PwC analysis found that women in midlife are leaving the workforce at the fastest rate since the 1990s, with caring responsibilities cited as the primary factor. The Government Equalities Office estimates that time spent out of employment for caregiving costs women an average of £141,000 in lost earnings and pensions over a lifetime. Workforce statistics categorise this as "economic inactivity" when in reality these women are working harder than most people in full-time employment. The productivity crisis is hiding in plain sight.

Taking time off for a sick child is culturally acceptable. Taking time off because your mother can't be left alone after a hospital discharge somehow feels like you're pushing boundaries or straying into skiving territory. Flexible working policies exist on paper but applying them to elder care still carries stigma in many workplaces. A woman asking to leave early three times a week for her father's dialysis appointments risks being seen as unreliable. The same woman leaving early for school sports day three times a term is being a good parent. The double standard is rarely spoken but it's widely felt.

The mental toll shows up in health data. A 2023 Ipsos Caregiving Index found that 64% of carers reported deteriorating mental health, with women twice as likely to say they felt "constantly overwhelmed". The sandwich generation describes life as being "always on call", never fully present anywhere because there's always something else demanding attention. Sleep suffers. Relationships suffer. The future feels like a long tunnel with no visible end because elder care, unlike childcare, doesn't have a clear finish line. Children grow up and become independent. Parents decline until they don't.

A 2024 investigation by *The Times* found that families supporting both generations were spending an average of £18,000 per year on care-related costs the state doesn't cover: respite care, private physiotherapy, care home top-ups, tutoring for children with additional needs. Middle-income families felt the squeeze hardest because they earned too much to qualify for most support but not enough to absorb costs comfortably. One child, usually a daughter, ends up doing the majority of care while siblings contribute financially or emotionally but rarely practically. Resentment builds quietly. The carer sibling feels unsupported. The distant siblings feel they're doing what they can. Family therapy researchers at the Tavistock Institute noted in 2024 that elder care was now one of the top five reasons adult siblings sought mediation, often after years of accumulated tension exploding into open conflict.

Then there's the guilt. You hear and read about the endless amounts of it. Guilt that you're not spending enough time with your children because your elderly parents need you. Guilt that you're neglecting your parent because your child has a disaster or a setback. Guilt that you resent both of them, even though you love them. Guilt that you're failing at work because you're distracted by your upwards and downwards care responsibilities and mental load. Guilt that you're considering residential care because you can't cope. The system relies on this guilt to keep families absorbing labour the state won't fund. A colleague explained recently that when she finally arranged respite care for a weekend, the intake worker asked, almost casually, "And you're sure there's no family member who could help instead?" Good daughters, apparently, don't need respite.

WHERE CONFIDENCE ENTERS

Operating with precision under sustained pressure requires knowing the right words to use, the right points to press, the right moments to escalate. Recognising that you're entitled to ask for help from siblings, from employers, from the state, even when cultural conditioning says competent women cope alone and get on with it. Having the tools to make those asks clearly rather than emotionally.

LLMs can't remove the pressure, but they can remove some of the cognitive fog that stress creates, especially when you're spinning a lot of plates, because they can turn panic into preparation. A woman juggling a parent's hospital discharge and her teenager's GCSE appeal could ask a model to generate two separate action plans: one listing everything needed for a safe discharge (equipment, medications, follow-up appointments, funding applications), the other outlining the appeals process for exam results including deadlines, required evidence and how to phrase the case. Both tasks involve similar skills – gathering information, meeting bureaucratic standards – but doing them simultaneously while also working and sleeping poorly is where hitting your limit can occur. AI can hold the structure steady while you move between crises.

Someone trying to access Carer's Allowance while also managing Attendance Allowance for a parent could ask the model to explain how the two interact, what the income thresholds are, whether one affects the other. The rules change frequently and eligibility depends on precise circumstances. Getting it wrong can mean losing benefits you qualified for or being overpaid and facing demands for repayment. Clarity prevents expensive mistakes.

Workplace negotiations benefit from preparation. A woman who needs flexible hours to manage caring responsibilities could ask an LLM to draft a proposal that cites the correct sections of employment law, outlines how the arrangement would work practically and addresses likely objections pre-emptively. The confidence to ask for accommodation increases dramatically when you're holding a well-structured document rather than hoping you'll find the right words in a stressful meeting.

Family communication improves with better tools. The sandwich generation often finds itself translating between generations and systems: explaining medical situations to elderly parents who don't understand, updating siblings who live far away, coordinating with schools and GPs and social workers. An LLM can draft clear, factual updates for a family WhatsApp group that inform without overwhelming, propose practical task-sharing rather than vague offers of "let me know if I can help", even generate agenda points for family meetings so conversations stay focused rather than devolving into emotion.

Every minute reclaimed from administrative chaos is a minute restored to paid work, rest or actual caregiving rather than paperwork about caregiving. The London School of Economics' Centre for Women, Peace and Security described "care-time poverty" as one of the most significant but least quantified gender inequalities. When technology helps redistribute time, it addresses equity as much as efficiency.

CHILDREN WITH COMPLEX NEEDS

Raising any child demands huge reserves of resilience. Raising one with complex health, developmental or educational needs demands stamina that borders on superhuman necessity. There's the intensity and relentlessness of care along with the loneliness of experiencing something most of your parenting peers probably aren't. There's also the sheer administrative weight associated with the support you need to seek that can exhaust even the most capable parents. SEN, EHCP, CAMHS, DLA, IEP – the acronyms become a second language few are taught, but most can't afford to ignore.

The scale is significant. In the UK around 1.5 million pupils, roughly 17% of all children, are identified as having special educational needs, according to the Department for Education's 2024 statistics. Globally, UNICEF estimates that over 240 million children live with some form of disability. Behind most of these statistics is usually a woman managing phone calls, juggling assessments, chasing referrals, compiling evidence, writing the same information repeatedly on different forms for different departments.

Unpaid labour for carers often stretches into irreversible invisible hours. For example, Carers UK reports that unpaid carers suffer an average earnings penalty of around £5,000 a year, rising to £8,000 a year after six years of caring. They also estimate that about 2.6 million carers have left work altogether to provide care. Families with disabled children face especially acute pressures: research suggests their pension deficits could reach £138,000 over a lifetime if caring prevents a return to paid employment. The combination of generous time commitment, reduced earnings and a forced exit from employment turns emotional strain into a long-term economic cost.

Beyond the numbers and the economics, there's the constant negotiation with systems that treat expertise as the preserve of professionals, not parents. Every interaction feels like a test. Assessments turn adversarial. Language gets coded. Entitlements hide behind legal phrasing. Eligibility thresholds are hard to interpret. A missed deadline or poorly worded application delays support for months. Parents document everything, anticipate resistance, become case managers in systems that, let's be honest, make very little sense.

LLMs help through decoding and translating. A parent can upload a 60-page EHCP draft and ask the model what's missing based on statutory requirements. It can surface gaps in provision, identify inconsistent language, suggest phrasing that aligns with official criteria. Walking into a review meeting prepared rather than overwhelmed changes the dynamic considerably.

In the UK, the application for Disability Living Allowance, currently a 60-question form notorious for its complexity, becomes more manageable when AI helps draft clear, factual responses that capture key details and avoid common pitfalls. It can simulate a local authority appeal process, letting parents rehearse arguments calmly before facing a tribunal panel. It can convert council jargon into plain English or generate evidence checklists that strengthen claims.

Professionals stay essential to the process. What changes is that parents can participate as informed equals rather than desperate petitioners. When parents ask sharper questions, meetings become more efficient. Professionals get better information up front. Children receive interventions faster. The Children's Commissioner's 2023 report identified delayed SEN assessments as one of the top five drivers of educational inequality in England. Shortening delays even by weeks changes trajectories.

The OECD's 2023 report on Inclusive Growth and Disability estimated that each year of delayed or inadequate support for a child with special educational needs translates into lower lifetime earnings and higher social care costs later. Early, sustained intervention, often unlocked by parents who persistently ask, yields a return of up to £6 for every £1 invested. Confidence in this bracket is fiscal strategy as much as advocacy.

AI can't interpret nuance or empathy. It can reproduce bias or give false reassurance. Parents shouldn't use models to diagnose, predict or litigate alone. But as a preparatory layer, a research assistant, translator and rehearsal partner, the technology redistributes power in a space long defined by asymmetry. It turns uncertainty into structure. It replaces late-night trawls through Facebook groups with a private, judgement-free space to ask questions about what should or could be done. The quiet value is time restored. Time to rest, to work, to parent without paperwork spilling across every surface at home.

THE MECHANICS OF JUST ASK IN CARE

Care situations demand a different kind of asking than negotiations over broadband bills or workplace salaries. The stakes are higher, the emotional weight heavier, the systems more deliberately opaque and frustrating. The Just Ask framework still applies, but adapted for contexts where exhaustion is the default state and where getting things wrong can mean a parent in crisis or a child without vital support.

- **Map the terrain.** Before you can ask effectively, you need to understand which system you're even dealing with. In elder care, that means knowing whether something falls under NHS acute care, council social care, or private provision. Upload council eligibility criteria into an LLM and ask it to explain in plain English what the thresholds actually mean. Feed in NHS Continuing Healthcare guidance and request a breakdown of the 12 assessment domains with examples of what evidence would strengthen a claim in each. For children with complex needs, map the statutory requirements for EHCPs or DLA applications so you know what must legally be provided versus what's discretionary. The value here is avoiding the trap most carers fall into: assuming the first person you speak to has given you complete information. They haven't, not because they're malicious but because systems are fragmented and individual caseworkers only see their small piece. AI can scan multiple policy documents simultaneously and highlight contradictions or gaps. A woman preparing for her father's care assessment could ask a model to compare what the council website says about eligibility with what the Care Act 2014 actually requires. The discrepancies are often revealing.

- **Frame the value.** Care asks work best when they're framed around outcomes rather than emotions. "My mother can't cope" is easy to dismiss as subjective. "My mother has fallen three times in six weeks, can't manage stairs safely and has missed medications on these documented dates" is harder to ignore. LLMs can help translate messy, emotional situations into the clinical language that unlocks funding. Upload notes from the last three months of your parent's decline and ask the model to organise them into categories that match CHC assessment criteria: cognition, behaviour, psychological needs, mobility, nutrition. For workplace flexibility requests, frame the ask around maintaining productivity rather than personal need. An LLM can draft a proposal that shows exactly how flexible hours would work in practice, which meetings you'd attend remotely, how handovers would happen and what your availability would be. Employers respond better to clear plans than to desperate pleas.

- **Rehearse.** Some of the hardest conversations in caregiving aren't with bureaucrats but with family members. Telling a parent they can't live alone any more. Asking siblings to contribute financially or practically. Informing an employer you need to reduce hours due to your increased caregiving needs. These conversations go wrong not because people are unkind but because emotions override clarity. Roleplay them with an LLM first. Ask it to simulate a resistant parent who insists they're fine. Practise responding calmly when the model pushes back with "I don't need help" or "You're overreacting". Try different phrasings until you find language that preserves dignity while stating facts. Do the same for sibling conversations. Ask the model to play the distant brother who thinks you're being dramatic. Rehearse responses to "Can't you just cope a bit longer?" or "Why don't you look into council services?" so you're not blindsided by dismissiveness in the actual conversation. Medical appointments benefit enormously from rehearsal. Consultants often speak in jargon and move quickly through appointments. Upload previous discharge notes and ask an LLM to generate five critical questions you should ask at the next appointment. Practise asking them confidently, not apologetically. Rehearse what to say if the consultant brushes you off or tries to end the meeting before you've got clarity.

- **Structure the ask.** Care assessments, funding applications, workplace flexibility proposals – they all work better when structured clearly. An LLM can take your scattered notes and organise them into the format that matters to the person receiving them. For a council care assessment, structure information around: current situation, safety concerns, care tasks currently being done by family (with hours quantified), what's needed, what the consequences are if support isn't provided. Lead with facts, support with evidence, end with a clear request. For CHC appeals, structure matters legally. The decision letter will cite specific reasons for rejection. Your appeal needs to address each point systematically, with evidence. AI can analyse the rejection letter, identify the weak arguments, and draft an appeal structure that tackles them in order. Include relevant case law, cite the National Framework, attach supporting evidence from medical professionals. The structure signals you're serious and informed, which changes how the appeal is handled.

- **Iterate.** Care situations rarely resolve in one attempt. CHC claims get rejected and need appeals. Council assessments initially offer inadequate hours. Employers deny flexibility requests. Each iteration teaches you something about what works. Keep notes, feed them into your LLM, ask what to adjust for next time. A rejected CHC claim might have failed because you described needs in lay terms rather than clinical language. The model can flag this and help you reframe for the appeal. Iteration also applies to family dynamics. The first time you ask siblings for help might go badly. They deflect, make vague promises, change the subject. Feed that conversation into an LLM and ask how to structure the next attempt more effectively. Perhaps you need to make the ask more specific: "Can you take Dad to his Tuesday appointments for the next three months?" rather than "Can you help more?" Maybe you need to frame it around fairness: "I'm doing 20 hours a week, here's the breakdown. What can each of you take on?"

- **Scale influence.** When one carer successfully navigates CHC funding, that knowledge spreads. When one parent wins a DLA appeal, others learn the tactics. Share what works, not just in your immediate circle but in online communities, support groups, local networks. The tactics that help you decode a care home contract might help dozens of others facing the same deliberately confusing clauses. Collectively, when enough carers start asking informed questions, systems begin to shift. Councils that routinely under-assessed care needs find themselves facing more challenges. NHS Trusts that reflexively rejected CHC claims discover families arriving with properly structured appeals citing case law. The individual act of asking confidently creates systemic pressure that benefits everyone behind you.

- **Care-specific adjustments.** Unlike workplace or financial negotiations, care-asking often happens when you're already depleted. You're negotiating for your parent from a hospital corridor between shifts. You're filling out DLA forms at midnight after a full day of work and parenting. The mechanics need to accommodate exhaustion. Batch the work when possible. Dedicate one session to gathering all documents and uploading them to an LLM. Let the model do the initial analysis while you make dinner or sleep. Come back to review its output when you have capacity. Break big tasks (like EHCP applications) into smaller pieces spread across days rather than trying to do everything in one sitting. Use AI to hold the structure steady across multiple sessions. You don't need to remember where you left off – the conversation history tracks it. Ask the model to set reminders for deadlines. "I have six weeks to appeal this decision, create a timeline with weekly milestones and tell me what to do each week." Caregiving often involves juggling multiple parallel processes with different deadlines. Offload the tracking to technology so your brain can focus on what you're asking for. Most importantly, recognise when to stop preparing and just act. Analysis paralysis is real when you're exhausted. An 80% prepared ask that actually gets made beats a 100% perfect ask that never leaves your drafts folder because you collapsed before finishing it. Use AI to get you to "good enough" faster, then execute.

FIVE CARE-RELATED SCENARIOS TO THINK ABOUT

Care situations are chaotic by nature, full of urgent decisions made with incomplete information while exhausted. These five scenarios show how preparation converts chaos into clarity, not by making care easy – nobody can do that – but by making the administrative maze slightly less punishing.

1. THE CHC NAVIGATOR

Scenario: A woman's mother was assessed for NHS Continuing Healthcare and rejected, despite significant health needs following a stroke. The decision letter cited "primarily social care needs" without clear justification. The family faced care home fees of £68,000 per year they couldn't sustain. She uploaded the rejection letter, her mother's medical records and the NHS CHC National Framework into a private LLM. The model identified three weak points in the reasoning: the assessment had under-scored mobility needs, hadn't properly considered cognition after the stroke and had applied the wrong threshold for behaviour. The LLM drafted an appeal structure that addressed each point systematically, suggested which medical evidence to obtain from the consultant and generated questions to ask the Continuing Healthcare coordinator. The appeal succeeded. The family saved £68,000 annually and the mother received appropriate health-led care.

How to use it: Upload rejection letters alongside policy frameworks and medical evidence. Ask the model to identify gaps between what the assessor claimed and what the evidence shows. Request a structured appeal that tackles each rejection reason in order, with space to insert specific supporting evidence. The model can't win the appeal for you, but it can ensure your case is presented in a structure and language that the system can't easily dismiss.

2. THE SIBLING MEDIATOR

Scenario: A woman in her late forties was providing all care for her elderly father while three siblings offered sympathy but no practical help. Resentment was building, family relationships were fracturing. She used an LLM to draft a family meeting agenda that quantified the current situation: 25 hours per week of care tasks broken down by category, £400 monthly out-of-pocket costs, three workplace conflicts from leaving early for emergencies. The model generated three options for sharing the load: a care rota, financial contribution for paid respite, or each sibling taking one specific responsibility (medications, finances, medical appointments, weekend care). The tone was factual rather than accusatory. The meeting shifted from defensive deflection to practical problem-solving. Two siblings took on specific tasks, one contributed financially, and the weekly burden dropped by 40%.

How to use it: Ask the model to help you quantify invisible labour. List everything you do, estimate hours, calculate costs. Then request three concrete options for redistribution that siblings could actually commit to. The structure removes emotion and makes it impossible for others to vaguely promise to "help more" without specifying how. Siblings respond better to clear requests than to exhausted meltdowns.

3. THE WORKPLACE NEGOTIATOR

Scenario: A woman needed to reduce her hours from full-time to four days per week to manage her mother's care and her daughter's CAMHS appointments. She worried about being seen as uncommitted or losing career progression. She used an LLM to draft a flexible working request that cited established policy and outlined exactly how responsibilities would be covered on her day off, proposed a three-month trial and included data showing how performance metrics had remained strong despite the strain. The proposal was three pages, professional and left nothing ambiguous. Her employer approved it within two weeks. A year later, she was promoted, the trial having demonstrated that productivity matters more than physical presence.

How to use it: Ask the model to draft a formal flexible working request that includes legal basis and practical details and addresses employer concerns pre-emptively. Structure it as a business proposal rather than a personal favour request. Include how handovers will work, which meetings you'll attend remotely, what your core hours will be. Employers approve specificity; they reject vagueness.

4. THE ASSESSMENT PREPARER

Scenario: A man's father was being assessed for council-funded care after multiple falls. Previous assessments had resulted in minimal support because the father, proud and determined, downplayed his needs during the meetings. This time, the son prepared differently. He kept a four-week diary of every fall, every missed medication, every meal skipped, every unsafe moment. He uploaded it to an LLM and asked it to organise the information into categories matching the Care Act 2014 eligibility criteria: wellbeing, safety, nutrition, managing the home. The model produced a two-page summary with specific dated examples in each category. At the assessment, the son handed it to the assessor at the start. Even when his father minimised things in conversation, the documented evidence was there. The care package doubled from four hours to nine hours per week.

How to use it: Start documenting before the assessment happens. Even two weeks of notes makes a difference. Ask the model to categorise your evidence according to whatever framework the assessment uses. Present it professionally. Assessors are trained to hear people downplay needs, either from pride or confusion. Evidence on paper is harder to dismiss than verbal claims.

5. THE HOSPITAL DISCHARGE ADVOCATE

Scenario: A woman's mother was declared medically fit after pneumonia and told discharge would happen the next day. But her home wasn't safe and the mother was weak, confused and couldn't manage stairs. The daughter had 18 hours to figure out what support existed. She uploaded the discharge letter and NHS intermediate care guidance into an LLM and asked what she was entitled to. The model explained reablement services (up to six weeks' funded support), outlined how to request a safe-discharge assessment and drafted questions to ask the discharge team: What equipment is being provided? Who assesses for reablement? What happens after six weeks? She went to the discharge meeting prepared. The team, used to families who don't know what to ask for, arranged two weeks of intermediate care, delivered mobility equipment and booked a follow-up care needs assessment. The mother went home safely instead of into crisis.

How to use it: Hospital discharge happens fast and often over weekends when support is minimal. Keep NHS discharge guidance saved somewhere accessible. The moment discharge is mentioned, upload the paperwork and ask the model what services should be offered. Generate a list of questions before the discharge meeting. Medical teams assume families will accept whatever is offered; asking informed questions changes what gets provided. Six hours of preparation can prevent six months of crisis.

PUSHBACK AND LIMITS

Most often, expanded care obligations land in the tricky part of life where you're already juggling a lot. It's a time where emotions and stress blur, and it's a time where, if we're honest, you need more things to worry about like a hole in the head. AI can only support to a point. It can help you get organised and understand the rules and policies of the alien worlds you're stepping into, but it can't take away the emotional toll or the structural failures that make care so exhausting to navigate in the first place. It can't create bandwidth you don't have or compensate for the underfunded systems stretched beyond capacity.

Preparation is useful, but it doesn't replace professional expertise. A model may help you understand the language in a care assessment, but it won't tell you whether your parent is safe at home, or whether a care home is under safeguarding review. It can summarise legal documents, but it isn't a solicitor. It can explain benefit eligibility, but it isn't accountable when the advice is outdated or incomplete. Care decisions often require a blend of law, money, health, risk, family history and emotion: terrain no predictive model can grasp and take off your plate entirely.

Privacy deserves particular mention here, as finding support with care involves some of the most sensitive information we ever hold about another person. Uploading documents to digital tools, even private ones, creates a trail you can't fully control. It is so important to anonymise everything. Scams targeting elderly people already exploit voice-cloning and impersonation capabilities, and breaches of care-related software have exposed deeply personal information. Treat every upload as if it may one day be seen by eyes it wasn't meant for; be diligent about removing sensitive or identifying information.

I worry there's also a cultural risk of shifting responsibility in the wrong direction. Once a system knows carers have better tools, it becomes tempting for institutions to offload even more on them. We've seen this pattern with online banking, energy portals and universal credit systems – efficiency for the provider, extra labour for the public. Care is already propped up by unpaid work, disproportionately done by women. Technology must lighten that load, not expand it.

And finally, confidence can become a double-edged sword. The more prepared families are, the more adversarial the relationship with professionals can feel. Social workers, GPs and assessors are operating under their own extreme pressures. Turning up armed with AI-generated arguments may strengthen your position, but it can also strain collaboration. Rubbing humans up the wrong way is never going to be helpful long term. The art is knowing when to push harder and when to defer to the professional in front of you, who's also navigating a broken system.

WHY CARE MATTERS

Care shapes the rhythm of daily life far more than we tend to admit. It determines who can work, who can study, who can rest, who burns out and who keeps the world turning quietly in the background. And because most care happens at home

– invisibly, unpaid and largely absorbed by families – it rarely appears in the places where powerful people gather or where care package budgets are set.

If more carers had the confidence, language and support to challenge opaque systems, the ripple effects would reach far beyond individual households. Councils would face better-prepared applicants, which would push them to be more efficient. NHS Trusts would hear clearer evidence. Benefit systems would encounter more families who clearly understand their rights. When more people turn up with questions and insights shaped by preparation rather than panic and agitation, the systems themselves begin to shift. Not overnight, but steadily, and in ways that become difficult to ignore.

This matters economically too. Unpaid care already keeps the country functioning. When carers can navigate the maze more efficiently, they lose less income, sustain their careers for longer and protect their own future stability. That strengthens households, not just budgets. It keeps more women attached to the workforce. It reduces the long-term costs of poorly supported families. A care system that people can actually use is an economic engine, not a drain.

And then there's the human layer, which never appears in government spreadsheets. When the administrative pressure eases, even slightly, carers get back some of the energy needed for the parts of care that matter most – dignity, patience, humour, kindness. AI tools don't replace that. They make room for it.

The shift begins with everyday moments: a daughter asking for clearer discharge notes, a son querying an assessment that doesn't reflect reality, a sibling planning care with fewer arguments because everyone finally understands what's involved. Small asks, multiplied across millions of households, have the potential to change the texture of care in this country.

What emerges is an approach to care that is more transparent, less punishing, more shareable and less lonely. A world where carers aren't expected to hold impossible amounts of knowledge in their heads and a world where the answers are easier to find.

CHAPTER EIGHT: EYES OPEN

WEAPONS OF MASS CONFIDENCE

So here we are: nearly time to wrap this all up, and if you've reached this far, you'll have spotted the theme that underpins everything. My firm view is that confidence is not a soft accessory or a personality trait, nor is it something you can nail by watching a few TED Talks. It is structural. It's quite literally a construct of the system. It shapes how women move through life and this spans everything, but especially work, health, money, relationships, care and showing up in public life. It shapes whose voice lands and whose gets tuned out. It even shapes the way entire economies grow, or stall.

Layer AI on top of that, and you get something wholly new. Here's a technology that can scan, summarise, role-play, translate, rewrite and rehearse at a speed no human can match. A tool that, in the right hands and used with a healthy dose of common sense, can help women convert hesitation into questions, and questions into better outcomes. It's a crazy kind of confidence accelerator that none of us saw coming or asked for, but now it's firmly here we should take full advantage of it.

At the same time as all this potential explodes for women, there is another story running directly alongside it, and if we're realistic, it's a scarier one for women than men. Generative AI is already being used to create deepfake abuse that overwhelmingly targets women, to automate jobs that women hold in disproportionate numbers and to entrench stereotypes in the images, words and translations it produces. It is already reshaping global power in ways that I imagine feel rather exciting if you're sitting in a boardroom, and frightening if you sit at the sharp end of a precarious work situation, or in a world where you're already on the front line fighting against engrained prejudice.

If *Weapons of Mass Confidence* is going to earn its title, it has to be honest about both sides, so this chapter and my closing reflections will attempt to sit in that tension: the upside of millions of women using AI as a rehearsal room and for added research muscle; the downside of increasingly powerful systems in our lives that are built on scraped labour and content, shaky regulation, questionable ownership and a long history of ignoring women altogether. I am going to sidestep making the definitive call on whether AI is good or bad, because I think we all know the answer is: both. For me, the provocation is what happens if women become fluent in it… and what happens if they do not?

PART ONE: THE TOOLS CAN TURN

The promise sounds simple enough: use AI to level the playing field. Research faster, prepare better, ask smarter questions, push for improved outcomes. For millions of women, these tools are already delivering measurable wins. But there's a question we can't lose sight of: who controls these tools, and what happens when their interests don't align with yours?

The easy-to-ignore reality is that ChatGPT, Claude, Gemini and every other LLM you're using aren't neutral utilities. They're products built by corporations with shareholders, growth targets and commercial partnerships. And over time, those partnerships are increasingly likely to include the very institutions you're trying to negotiate with.

CORPORATE CAPTURE: WHEN YOUR PREP PARTNER SWITCHES SIDES

In early 2024, OpenAI announced a partnership with several major financial institutions to develop "industry-specific" versions of ChatGPT. The pitch to banks was straightforward: help us train models that understand your sector better. The reality is more questionable: banks are now actively shaping how AI responds to financial queries, with access to anonymised user data that reveals exactly how customers prepare for negotiations.

Think about what this means in practice. You spend an evening using ChatGPT to research mortgage rates, compare offers and draft negotiation scripts. That conversation, even if technically "private", contributes to the training data that teaches the model how borrowers think. Meanwhile, your bank is using enterprise AI trained on millions of similar conversations to predict exactly which customers are likely to switch, what objections they'll raise and which counter-offers will make them stay.

Eventually it'll become clear it's far from a level playing field. It's an arms race where one side has vastly more resources and you're inadvertently supplying intelligence to the opposition.

It's reasonable to anticipate this will repeat across a wide range of sectors. Insurance companies are exploring partnerships with AI providers to better understand customer behaviour and risk assessment. Healthcare technology firms are integrating LLMs into patient management systems, pitched to improve care but also possibly to identify "high-usage" patients who ask too many questions or challenge diagnoses. Retailers are using AI to optimise dynamic pricing based on how informed shoppers appear to be.

This stuff is going on already. Google's integration with financial comparison sites means your research behaviour feeds directly into advertising algorithms that then target you with "personalised" offers designed to look competitive while still protecting their profit margins. Amazon's AI analyses your browsing patterns to adjust prices in real time, showing different costs to different users based on perceived willingness to pay. It's likely your utility providers are exploring AI-powered customer-service systems trained to identify which customers will accept price increases and which need to be offered retention deals.

The most insidious part isn't the technology itself but the asymmetry it creates. When you use a free AI tool, you're the product. Your questions, your concerns, your negotiation strategies become data points that train systems designed to extract maximum value from you. Corporations will soon be studying them at scale to build better defences, if they aren't already. I draw parallels to Facebook, Instagram and all the social platforms... there's no such thing as a free app.

Some AI companies are pitching "ethical" alternatives: paid tiers with stronger privacy commitments, enterprise versions that don't train on your data, open-source models you can run locally. But these solutions widen another gap. Women with disposable income get the reassurance of being able to tap into more private versions of AI assistance. Everyone else gets surveillance dressed up as support.

Right now the regulatory landscape offers little protection and is struggling to move at the pace of technology. Data protection laws like GDPR were designed for an earlier era and struggle to keep pace with how AI systems learn and share information. Most terms of service are deliberately vague about what happens to your conversation history. Even "private" modes offered by some platforms come with caveats buried in the fine print. And because these are global platforms operating across jurisdictions, enforcement is patchy at best.

There's no easy solution here, but on an individual level at least, the strategy needs to be one of common sense and pragmatism, another parallel to using social media. Anonymise all information before uploading anything personal, and use paid versions with clear privacy policies for genuinely sensitive negotiations. Assume that anything you put into a free tool could eventually surface in some aggregated form or other. Treat AI as you would any powerful but untested work ally: useful for certain tasks, dangerous for others, never given your complete confidence.

THE SUBSCRIPTION TRAP: POWER BEHIND PAYWALLS

In March 2024, OpenAI changed its pricing structure. ChatGPT Plus, the paid tier, gives access to more powerful models, longer conversation histories and priority access during peak times. Free users were relegated to older, slower versions with tighter usage limits. By mid-year, Claude and Gemini had followed suit. The signals were clear: the most capable AI was moving behind paywalls.

On the surface, this seems reasonable, especially for a new technology that must cost billions to run. Companies need revenue, and users who pay should get better service. But look a bit closer at what's actually being gated and you discover it's not just speed or convenience, it is also capability. The free versions struggle with complex documents, hit token limits quickly, restrict your activity during peak traffic windows and can't access real-time information as reliably. For casual users, comparing long-haul travel routing or searching for how to object to a traffic penalty, this barely matters. For a woman trying to decode a 60-page care home contract or prepare for a high-stakes salary negotiation by triangulating earnings data in her field of expertise, it's possible she's getting lower-quality output.

To make a point – a solicitor can probably afford £20 per month for AI tools that save hours of research, whereas a single mother working two jobs and caring for an elderly parent possibly can't. The woman who needs these tools most, the one juggling impossible logistics with no spare bandwidth, is exactly the one priced out of the versions that would actually help most.

We know this is how it works, of course. Freemium business models are designed to create dependency and then monetise it. You start using a free tool, integrate it into your workflow, and come to rely on it. Then the capabilities you've been using get moved to a paid tier. You can either pay up or lose ground to people who do.

Dig a bit deeper and you'll discover the tiering goes further than basic versus premium. Enterprise versions of these tools, sold to corporations and institutions, come with features individuals will never access. Bulk processing, advanced analytics, custom training on proprietary data. A local council using enterprise AI to manage benefit applications has tools far more sophisticated than the citizen trying to navigate the same system with a free ChatGPT account. A bank's customer retention team has AI that can analyse thousands of conversations to identify patterns and optimise responses. You're using consumer-grade tools to negotiate with professionals using military-grade systems.

Educational access provides another misalignment around fairness. I've seen reports that some AI companies offer free or discounted access to students and educators, which sounds generous until you consider how this contributes to advancing the few, not the many. Follow this through and we'll see young women at university develop AI fluency early, first integrating it into their study habits and then carrying those skills into professional life. Women who left education before these tools existed, particularly those without degrees, start from further behind and have fewer supported pathways to catch up.

Geographic paywalls compound the problem of lack of fairness. Many AI tools price subscriptions in US dollars without adjusting for local purchasing power, making a £20-equivalent monthly fee manageable in London but far less attainable in cities like Lagos or Manila. The global digital gender divide means women in lower-income economies often have the least access to paid digital tools, despite standing to benefit significantly from them. My takeaway is that the Confidence Gap gets redrawn along economic and financial lines.

The counter-argument is that open-source alternatives solve this – models you can download and run locally without subscriptions or data sharing. In theory, yes. In practice, running these requires technical knowledge most people don't have. I wouldn't have the first clue where to start. Open source is a solution for technically sophisticated early adopters, not for exhausted women trying to navigate bureaucracy late at night.

Speaking to the commentators about this, many say that it's possible, even likely, that paywalls will get higher as these tools become more valuable. The question becomes whether women with resources subsidise access for those without, whether governments step in with public alternatives or whether we reluctantly find ourselves accepting that AI-enabled confidence becomes another privilege marker, available to some and denied to others.

THE REGULATION RISK: PROTECTING CORPORATIONS, NOT CONSUMERS

In 2024 the European Union adopted its landmark AI legislation, the Artificial Intelligence Act, with one of its central aims to protect individuals from manipulative AI use. While the law primarily targets providers and systems that influence consumer-facing services such as credit, employment and public administration, a more subtle implication is how it could change the power dynamic in consumer–institution negotiations. For example, if a bank or insurer deploys an AI model to steer negotiation outcomes, it may face stricter transparency and disclosure requirements, potentially making it harder for individual consumers to rely on AI tools themselves without raising questions about fairness or undue influence.

Similar regulatory discussions are happening in the UK, US and Australia. The language is always about fairness, transparency and preventing abuse, but it is essential we pay attention to who's actually writing these rules. Financial services industry groups, healthcare provider associations, insurance company coalitions – they all have dedicated lobbying arms and legal teams actively shaping these regulations, whereas the everyday consumers have advocacy groups operating on shoestring budgets.

One of the more interesting conversations happening around the EU's AI legislation is how far these new transparency rules might stretch. The act is mainly aimed at companies using AI, especially when it shapes decisions about credit, employment or public services, but some voices in Brussels are now asking whether there should also be disclosure when AI is used on the *other* side of the table. In practice, that could mean consumers having to reveal that they used an AI tool to draft a complaint or prepare for a negotiation, supposedly to prevent unfair advantage or fraud. Nothing like that is written into law, but it even being floated shows how quickly the balance of power could shift. Imagine having to tell a company you've done your homework before you're allowed to challenge them... It sounds absurd, but it's genuinely part of the current debate.

Another idea doing the rounds is the introduction of mandatory "fairness audits" for AI tools that might support people in disputes or negotiations. On paper it sounds fine, because who's against fairness? But the moment you dig into it, the whole thing becomes a bit slippery. Who exactly gets to run these audits, and what counts as "fair"? If the benchmark quietly becomes "Does this tool help consumers push back or pay less?" then anything that actually works gets flagged as a problem. What starts as an audit framework quickly morphs into a neat way of spotting and clipping the wings of effective consumer-advocacy tools.

Data protection regulations, meant to safeguard privacy, are also being stretched in concerning directions. Some proposals would classify AI-assisted negotiation as "automated decision-making" requiring explicit consent from both parties. This would effectively ban the use of AI to prepare for conversations unless the other side agrees. Try asking your mortgage broker: "Is it okay if I used ChatGPT to prepare for this meeting?" Watch how quickly the dynamic shifts.

Employment law is another frontier. Several jurisdictions are considering whether using AI to draft resignation letters, negotiate severance or challenge workplace decisions constitutes misrepresentation if not disclosed. The argument goes that employers deserve to know if they're negotiating with a person or a "person plus AI". But this framing treats AI as a suspicious advantage rather than what it actually is: a research and preparation tool, no different from reading a book or consulting a friend.

All this is on the horizon, not yet set in stone. But should it become a reality, it's reasonable to assume the effect of these regulations would be fairly immediate. Even if disclosure requirements don't pass, the mere discussion of them makes people nervous. Women already second-guess whether they're allowed to advocate for themselves. Adding legal uncertainty about whether using AI is somehow improper just reinforces hesitation. The goal of these proposals, whether stated or not, is to make informed asking feel risky enough that people don't bother.

What we do know is that the race is already well underway. If regulations restricting consumer AI use arrive before enough women have adopted these tools and seen the results, I worry that the window will close. The tactics that work today become legally risky tomorrow. And the institutions that profit from confusion will have successfully defended their turf using the language of consumer protection.

WHERE THIS LEAVES US

We can only work with what's concrete – the fact these tools exist and they work. But the reminder ultimately is that they're not yours, they're rented from corporations with competing interests. They're increasingly expensive, pricing out some of the women who need them most. And they're under regulatory threat from industries that want to preserve information asymmetry.

This doesn't mean we should be abandoning them. It means we use them strategically, with eyes open about their limitations and whose interests they ultimately serve. It means pushing for genuine data protection that favours individuals over institutions. It means recognising that the window for taking advantage of these tools may be narrower than we'd like.

The counter-revolution isn't coming. It's here. The question is whether enough women adopt these tactics quickly enough to reach critical mass before the defences fully lock into place. Because once the tools are captured, paywalled and regulated into submission, the Confidence Gap gets coded into the technology itself.

PART TWO: THE EQUITY PROBLEM WE'RE CREATING

There's an uncomfortable truth beneath every success story in this book. The woman who used AI to decode her father's care assessment and secure better funding? She had a laptop, reliable broadband and three quiet evenings to work through the process. The entrepreneur who rehearsed her investor pitch until it landed perfectly? She could afford the paid tier of Claude that lets you upload unlimited documents. The professional who negotiated a better redundancy package? She had the education to recognise jargon when she saw it and the confidence that comes from a lifetime of feeling entitled to ask questions.

AI-enabled confidence is stratifying opportunity in new and troubling ways. We're narrowing the Confidence Gap for some women while widening it for others. And if we're serious about what this technology means, we need to be honest about who it leaves behind.

THE CLASS DIVIDE GETS CODED

There's a surprising divide in device access in this country still. Research from the Joseph Rowntree Foundation and other charities shows that households in the lowest income quintile are far less likely to own a laptop or desktop, and rely far more on smartphones or pay-as-you-go data plans. Meanwhile, households in the top income quintile enjoy almost universal access to full devices and fixed broadband. Sure, a smartphone means you can join a Zoom call or open a PDF, but try negotiating your salary or decoding a 40-page council grant assessment on a cracked iPhone screen with a 2GB monthly allowance. Technically possible but practically pretty miserable.

The women most likely to benefit from AI tools are the ones who need them least. A recent University of Oxford study on digital inequality found that degree-educated women were four times more likely to have used generative AI than women without qualifications. The Chartered Institute of Personnel and Development reported in early 2025 that professional and managerial workers were twice as likely as those in routine occupations to have experimented with AI for work-related tasks.

We should also acknowledge what "access" actually requires beyond owning a device. The internet, reliable enough that you can use it freely rather than rationed. Digital literacy that extends beyond Facebook and WhatsApp. Most critically, perhaps, an educational foundation sufficient to spot when an AI output sounds plausible but potentially wrong. Confidence to experiment with unfamiliar tools without fear of breaking something or looking stupid. And time, perhaps the scarcest resource of all for women.

A 2024 investigation by *The Guardian* into the UK's digital divide found that women in social housing were significantly less likely to have home internet than those in owner-occupied properties, with cost cited as the primary barrier. Universal Credit claimants, 60% of whom are women, reported struggling to access online government services because of inadequate devices or connectivity.

The Trades Union Congress published an analysis in late 2024 showing that workers in the lowest-paid sectors, which skew towards retail, hospitality and care work, were least likely to have employer support for digital skills development, and these sectors employ women overwhelmingly. The women stacking shelves or changing care-home bed sheets get managed by AI-powered scheduling systems designed to extract maximum flexibility at minimum cost, but nobody offers them lunch-and-learn sessions on how AI could help them negotiate better pay or decode their zero-hours contracts.

Even when access exists, capability takes time to develop. The Centre for Ageing Better found that only 38% of women over 65 felt confident using new technology, compared to 52% of men in the same age bracket. These are the exact women navigating complex care systems, making pension decisions, writing wills and working through end-of-life planning either for themselves or with a loved one. I can't help but reflect that the demographic most in need of tools to decode bureaucracy is the one least equipped to use them.

The uncomfortable question nobody wants to voice: are we simply creating a new category of privilege? The AI-literate versus the AI-excluded. The women who can afford preparation versus those who continue winging it. The ones who know how to ask versus those who stay silent because they lack awareness that better questions even exist.

THE LANGUAGE BARRIER NOBODY MENTIONS

Here's another thing worthy of lingering on: these tools are phenomenally English-centric. Yes, ChatGPT and Claude support multiple languages technically, but they were trained predominantly on English-language internet content and they perform best – so most accurately and most usefully – when you interact with them in English.

The Pew Research Center found that 85% of global AI development and deployment was happening in English-speaking markets or contexts where English dominates as a business language. For the 1.5 billion women worldwide who speak little or no English, these tools range from marginally useful to entirely inaccessible.

Even within English-speaking countries, there are still language barriers to consider. In the UK, where roughly 8% of the population speaks English as a second language according to the 2021 census, many women from immigrant communities find these tools confusing or intimidating. The confidence to interrogate a council housing decision or challenge a GP's diagnosis requires speaking English with precision and fluency, and AI might not be geared to offer the same level of assistance.

A British Future study in 2024 on integration and digital inclusion found that women from South Asian and Eastern European communities were significantly less likely to use AI tools than white British women, even when access ceased to be a barrier. When you lack complete comfort with English, you struggle to judge when an AI output sounds plausible but wrong. That uncertainty alone makes the tools feel more risky than helpful.

The problem is clearly a global one. Women in francophone Africa, in Latin America, in South and Southeast Asia encounter AI tools built primarily for American and British users. The localisation right now is superficial at best. A woman in Lagos trying to use AI to understand Nigerian employment law will get responses filtered through an American legal framework unless she possesses the sophistication to prompt her way around that bias. Most people lack that skill. I certainly would.

It goes far beyond translation: cultural context, legal systems, social norms, institutional structures all vary wildly by region. AI trained on the English-speaking internet knows little about how Indian family courts work or how Brazilian pension systems function or what questions matter in a Kenyan healthcare setting. The tools claim global reach. The reality right now looks colonial. They work best for people who already operate in Western, English-speaking contexts.

Even within that narrow band, accent and dialect matter. AI transcription tools, voice assistants, anything involving speech recognition performs worse for speakers with regional or minority accents. A 2023 study from Stanford found that voice recognition error rates were nearly twice as high for speakers with strong regional accents compared to standard American English. If you're Scottish, Jamaican, or from certain parts of Northern England, the tools literally hear you less clearly.

There is, as always, an economic rationale to all this. Building robust AI capabilities in languages spoken by poorer populations lacks commercial attraction. There's no profit incentive to make these tools work brilliantly in Swahili or Bengali when the wealthy, more globally commercial markets speak English. The result becomes predictable: the Confidence Gap contracts for anglophone professional women and expands for everyone else.

It's important for me to again be honest about whose problems this book sets out to address. A woman in rural India worrying about secure drinking water and basic education for her daughters faces concerns that make negotiating a better mortgage rate or preparing for a workplace salary review look like the privilege they totally are.

The Confidence Gap this book tackles exists primarily as a wealthy nation problem. It emerges because women in developed economies have enough baseline security to care about how and where they can optimise and improve aspects of their lives. You need a certain level of income and stability before "asking for more" becomes the primary constraint on your life. For far too many women globally, the big constraints are still structural poverty, limited legal rights, inadequate access to education and healthcare and, appallingly, genuine threats to physical safety.

These issues sit outside the frame of what this book can solve. It would be total madness to pretend that better AI prompts will fix global inequality or that women in Lahore should prioritise learning to use ChatGPT over securing education. But to call it what it is: AI-enabled confidence represents a first-world solution to a first-world problem.

I've spent most of my time focused on the individual and collective benefits, but there's an adjacent tension that emerges from progress that warrants highlighting – let's call it the brain drain element. The women in developing economies who do gain digital literacy and AI fluency often leave, moving to wealthier markets where those skills get valued and compensated. A Brookings Institution paper in 2024 noted that AI talent migration flows overwhelmingly from poorer to richer countries. The women who could potentially teach others and build local capacity instead get recruited away, leaving their communities further behind.

I close with all this because I think honesty is important and it highlights how complex progress can be. These tools remain worth using, but we should never find ourselves pretending they represent universal solutions. They're concentrating opportunity further in the places and populations that already have the most.

WHERE THIS LEAVES US

AI-enabled confidence works, but it works disproportionately for women who already had a few advantages under their belts, be that education, income, digital access, language fluency or reliable technology. Right now and in the immediate future, these prerequisites will exclude more women than they include.

So what needs to happen? Well, in an ideal world we'll push towards using these tools while simultaneously pushing for structural changes that would actually level the field. Free public digital literacy programmes and subsidised broadband, more device loans and grants for low-income families. Investment in developing robust AI capabilities in languages beyond English. Regulatory pressure on platforms to provide genuinely accessible versions rather than charity tiers that hobble functionality.

Use the tools if you can and find ways to share the tactics with women who might never discover them otherwise. But let's recognise the difference between individual empowerment and collective justice. The women being left behind by this AI revolution aren't just those who are failing to adopt. There are also women being failed by systems that were never designed with them in mind.

PART THREE: WHY WE DO IT ANYWAY

I feel I'm straying into less than optimistic territory to close. You might now be mulling on these reality checks and thinking – given all that, why bother?

Well, to put it frankly: because the alternative has been tested for generations and the results are in. Waiting for systems to fix themselves simply doesn't work. Nothing in this world is perfect, with the exception of dogs. Hoping institutions will voluntarily become transparent and fair doesn't work, nor does hoping the flaws in our societal structures will simply correct themselves.

What changes the equation is volume. When one woman asks an informed question and gets brushed off, that's an individual loss. When a hundred women in the same borough arrive at council meetings with the same level of preparation, citing the same policies, asking variations of the same pointed questions, that's a pattern institutions struggle to ignore. When thousands of women switch banks because retention offers suddenly look insultingly low compared to new customer rates, pricing teams notice. When GP surgeries across a region start encountering patients who've done their homework and expect substantive answers, the culture in those consulting rooms begins to shift.

In many ways, the maths here matters more than the sentiment. Research on social movements and behaviour change consistently shows that you don't need majority adoption to shift norms. You need somewhere between 25% and 30% of a population to adopt a new behaviour before it starts feeling inevitable rather than exceptional. We're nowhere near that threshold yet with AI-enabled confidence, but the trajectory suggests we could get there faster than previous technological shifts precisely because the barriers to adoption are lower than they were for, say, online banking or smartphone use.

The evidence base is building quietly. NHS Continuing Healthcare appeals are being won by families who've used AI to structure their cases properly, citing the National Framework with precision rather than pleading emotionally. Employment tribunals are seeing better-prepared claimants who've rehearsed their testimony and assembled their evidence coherently. Local authorities are approving care packages they would have rejected five years ago because families now arrive at assessments with documentation that meets statutory thresholds. These aren't flashy victories that make national headlines, but they're data points in a pattern that's already starting to emerge.

The backlash and counter-revolution we're also navigating through? They're proof of concept, aren't they. Banks don't redesign retention scripts unless the old ones are failing. Councils don't get defensive about informed residents unless those residents are actually winning. Institutions only adapt when threatened. The speed at which they're already adapting tells you how seriously they're taking this shift.

What becomes possible at scale goes beyond individual wins. When enough women negotiate salaries confidently and successfully, the stigma around asking eventually evaporates. It stops being coded as "aggressive" or "unfeminine" and becomes expected professional behaviour. When enough women challenge utility bills, pension statements and care home contracts, the companies maintaining those deliberately opaque systems face a choice: simplify or lose customers to competitors who already have.

This is how institutional behaviour changes. Not through goodwill or regulation alone, but through sustained economic and reputational pressure that makes the old way of operating too expensive to maintain.

Ultimately, the end goal here is to make this book obsolete. If every woman becomes completely literate in asking for what she deserves, if confidence gaps close entirely, if systems become so transparent that preparation becomes unnecessary because there's nothing left to decode, that would be the best possible outcome. Wouldn't that be brilliant?

But we're not there and the window is closing. Tools are being paywalled and regulated. The equity gaps are real and widening. The window is still open today, though. Right now, the leverage exists. The tactics work. The information is accessible. The question isn't whether the fight is fair. It never has been. The question is whether you're in it. And if you are, whether you're willing to bring others along. Because individual confidence is valuable, but collective confidence is transformative. When millions of women start asking informed questions across every domain, work and health and money and care and public life, the cumulative pressure becomes impossible to deflect. Systems adapt or collapse under the weight of informed scrutiny.

That's the weapon. Not AI itself, but what happens when enough women use it to stop accepting confusion as inevitable. When asking stops feeling risky and starts feeling ordinary. When confidence becomes so widespread that silence becomes the exception rather than the rule.

CLOSING: WHAT TO DO TOMORROW

You've read about the risks, the limitations, the equity problems we're creating while claiming progress. You know that the tools all come with corporate interests and that the women who need these advantages most are the ones least likely to get them. You know the window is narrowing.

So what now?

If you haven't already, make a start. Pick one thing that's been sitting on your mental list, the thing you've been putting off because it feels complicated or intimidating or like it'll take forever to sort out. The electricity bill that seems too high. The pension statement you don't understand. The GP appointment where you never ask the questions you mean to. The contract buried in jargon that you signed because you were bored of dealing with admin.

Take 30 minutes. Open ChatGPT or Claude or whichever tool you fancy trying. Paste in the relevant document, if you have one, or just describe the situation. Ask it to explain what you're looking at in plain language. Ask what questions you should be asking. Ask what your options are. Then do something with that information, even if it's just sending one email or making one phone call or writing down three questions for next time.

That's it. One task. Then tell someone else what you learned, preferably another woman who might face something similar. Not as a lecture or a tutorial, just as a "here's what I tried and it actually worked". Because tactics spread through networks faster than inspiration does, and right now we need tactics as well as enthusiasm.

Over the next few months, do that again. And again. Pick different problems, different situations. Notice what works and what doesn't. Notice which prompts get you useful answers and which ones lead nowhere. Notice when the AI sounds confident but wrong, and learn to spot that gap between plausibility and accuracy. Build your own informal mental playbook.

When you encounter the backlash, and you will, name it. Say it out loud to someone you trust. "I prepared really well for that meeting and my manager said I seemed over-rehearsed." "I asked informed questions at the GP and got told I was being difficult." "I challenged the quote and they made me feel like I was being unreasonable." Naming it makes it visible. Visible patterns become harder to sustain.

Teach younger women, the ones coming up behind you who are watching how you navigate these situations. Daughters, nieces, mentees, colleagues who are earlier in their careers or newer to these systems. Model asking questions and asking for more in life as normal behaviour. Let them see you prepare without apology, question without embarrassment, push back without guilt. What you normalise now becomes their baseline later.

This is how confidence spreads, through observation and repetition. Through seeing someone you know do something you thought was impossible, then realising it's just uncomfortable rather than actually forbidden.

The structural stuff matters too. Consider connecting your individual wins to bigger movements. Organisations like Citizens Advice, Which?, the Fawcett Society and Carers UK are already fighting for transparency and accountability in the systems you're navigating daily. Join them and amplify their work. Your personal victories and their institutional pressure work together. Neither succeeds alone.

Because here's what Weapons of Mass Confidence actually means. This isn't about AI making women "better" at navigating broken systems while leaving those systems intact. It's about enough women asking informed questions, backed by enough preparation, that the systems can't sustain their current level of brokenness. When opacity stops working as a strategy because too many people have learned to see through it, institutions have to adapt or collapse.

That's the future this book is pushing towards. One where the Permission Gap closes because permission stopped being required. Where silence is the exception rather than the rule. Where institutions expect informed questions and build their processes accordingly because trying to rely on confusion has become commercially unsustainable.

Just Ask isn't about being polite or seeking permission. It's about claiming power that's been deliberately withheld through systems designed to exhaust you into giving up. It's informed demanding, not hopeful requesting. It's preparation as a weapon, questions as leverage, confidence as collective force.

The confidence you build tomorrow compounds into leverage next month. The tactics you share next week accelerate someone else's adoption. The questions you ask next year make the same questions easier for whoever asks them after you. This is how gaps close and norms shift and systems bend under sustained pressure from people who decline to stay confused.

Now go and type something you have been avoiding. Then see where the answer takes you.

Start small. Start now.

Just Ask.

Kat Thomas is a multi-award-winning creative entrepreneur and communications leader. She has built and sold two successful businesses and recently founded her third, a new creative communications company specialising in public relations in the age of AI answers. With more than two decades leading global campaigns for major brands, Kat is known for her instinct for culture, audience insight and bold ideas that spark conversation. *Weapons of Mass Confidence* draws on her experience at the intersection of creativity, confidence and technology, exploring how AI could reshape women's power and potential in everyday life.

Publisher Information

Rowanvale Books provides publishing services to independent authors, writers and poets all over the globe. We deliver a personal, honest and efficient service that allows authors to see their work published, while remaining in control of the process and retaining their creativity. By making publishing services available to authors in a cost-effective and ethical way, we at Rowanvale Books hope to ensure that the local, national and international community benefits from a steady stream of good quality literature.

For more information about us, our authors or our publications, please get in touch.

www.rowanvalebooks.com
info@rowanvalebooks.com